S0-AEY-950

# Husband
# Father
# Worker

*Questions and Answers
About Saint Joseph*

Imprimi Potest:
Harry Grile, CSsR, Provincial
Denver Province, The Redemptorists

Published by Liguori Publications
Liguori, Missouri 63057

To order, call 800-325-9521, or visit liguori.org.

Copyright © 2012 Larry Toschi, José Antonio Bertolin, and Rick Sarkisian

All rights reserved. No part of this publication may be reproduced, stored in a retrieval system, or transmitted in any form or by any means—electronic, mechanical, photocopy, recording, or any other—except for brief quotations in printed reviews, without the prior written permission of Liguori Publications.

**Library of Congress Cataloging-in-Publication Data**

Toschi, Larry M.
 Husband, father, worker: questions and answers about Saint Joseph /
Larry Toschi, José Antonio Bertolin, and Rick Sarkisian—1st ed.
 p. cm.
 ISBN 978-0-7648-2097-7
 1. Joseph, Saint—Miscellanea. I. Bertolin, José Antonio. II. Sarkisian, Rick. III. Title.
 BS2458.T65 2011
 232.9'32—dc23
                    2011044859

Scripture quotations are from the *Revised Standard Version of the Bible*, copyright 1952 [2nd edition, 1971] by the Division of Christian Education of the National Council of the Churches of Christ in the United States of America. Used by permission. All rights reserved.

Pope John Paul II's *Redemptoris Custos* quotations are used with permission. Copyright Libreria Editrice Vaticana (© Libreria Editrice Vaticana 2012)

The English translation of the Collect of Saint Joseph from *The Roman Missal*, © 2010, International Commission on English in the Liturgy Corporation. All rights reserved.

Liguori Publications, a nonprofit corporation, is an apostolate of the Redemptorists. To learn more about the Redemptorists, visit Redemptorists.com.

Printed in the United States of America
15 14 13 12 11 / 5 4 3 2 1
First Edition

# Husband Father Worker

## Questions and Answers About Saint Joseph

Father Larry Toschi, OSJ
Father José Antonio Bertolin, OSJ
Rick Sarkisian, PhD

Liguori
LIGUORI, MISSOURI

# Contents

# Authors' Note

The original material of this book was published in Brazil as *100 Questões de Josefologia* by Father José Antonio Bertolin, OSJ, in 1999. Father Larry Toschi, OSJ, then translated, adapted, and supplemented this material, publishing a few questions each quarter under the title "Josephology 1A" in *Guardian of the Redeemer* magazine beginning in September 2000. Finally, Rick Sarkisian, PhD, reorganized and abridged the material, put it into a colloquial format, and further supplemented it with extensive practical applications, with the editorial collaboration of Father Toschi.

The authors thank Mike Phillips and Christopher Knuffke for their editorial insights, Sandy Huerta for transcription, and Debbie Druley for her valuable help in proofreading the text.

# Foreword

The husband of Mary and the chosen father of Jesus, Saint Joseph, is at the heart of the Holy Family and, indeed, the story of salvation itself. Churches and cathedrals have been named for him. Countless congregations, institutes, and societies profess a devotion to him. Indeed, Joseph is beloved and venerated by believers all around the world—certainly by me and, I hope, by you!

I wonder, though, how much do we really know about him?

The Bible portrays Joseph as a rugged, down-to-earth, hardworking man who was very involved in the day-to-day life of his family and his world.

It is my hope that every question and answer in this book will draw you closer to Joseph in your everyday life and help you understand the virtues that make him worthy of devotion while equipping you to demonstrate those virtues wherever God calls you in the home, the church, the workplace, and the world.

Join Father José Antonio Bertolin, Father Larry Toschi from the Oblates of Saint Joseph (my cousin), and me as we embark on the path of discovering who Saint Joseph is and the role he can play in our lives today.

RICK SARKISIAN, PhD

# Introduction

Most of us have only seen Saint Joseph in sacred art. While that makes it easier for us to grow in devotion to him, it also makes it hard to expand our thinking about Joseph, to think of him as a *real* person—a flesh-and-blood craftsman from Nazareth who experienced the same fears and joys we all face in our lives.

*Q* Why should we be interested in Joseph? After all, he's totally silent in Scripture.

*A* That's true. There are no words of Joseph recorded in Scripture, yet his silent life speaks volumes about love, obedience, integrity, and the value of good work.

*Q* Why should I pray to Joseph when I can go directly to Jesus?

*A* The saints—those holy ones who have already arrived at their heavenly home—offer a direct link to the merciful love of God. When asking for their help, we ask their intercession and entrust our needs to them. Just as we pray for the needs of those we know and love, Joseph will do the same for us as we seek his constant care.

# CHAPTER ONE

# Everyday Life
# in the Time of Joseph

**Q** **What does the name "Joseph" mean?**

**A** In biblical times, names were a lot more important than they are today, often describing the person's character or destiny. So it's significant that the name "Joseph" means "Yahweh increases" or "Yahweh makes grow." This is from the Latin *Ioseph(us)* and from the Hebrew (*Iehôsép*).

In Genesis 30:22–24, Jacob's wife, Rachel, gives her baby the name "Joseph" to recognize that God added to her the blessing of this son. Genesis 49:22 of the Vulgate reads: *Filius accrescens Ioseph*, "Joseph is a growing son," or "Joseph is a fruitful bough." Prior to the Second Vatican Council in the 1960s, this reading was used for the Votive Mass of Saint Joseph on Wednesdays to convey that, just as the Old Testament patriarch, Joseph, was blessed in his descendants, so, too, was Saint Joseph blessed by being chosen as father to Jesus, the fruit of Mary's womb.

## Q What was the geography of Israel when Joseph was born?

A Joseph was born in Palestine, where the country of Israel is located today, east of the Mediterranean Sea on a stretch of land about 150 miles by ninety miles. While this is a fertile area, it is also marked by desolate deserts and rocky hills ranging from 1,600 to 3,000 feet in elevation, running through regions known as Galilee, Samaria, and Judea.

In Joseph's time, just as today, the Sea of Galilee was of major importance. Fourteen miles long, seven miles wide, and 150 feet deep, it was one of the principal centers of life for Joseph's people, mainly for fishing.

The Jordan River was also important, winding more than 200 miles before emptying into the Dead Sea. The water is so salty it supports no type of life. Thus its name, "Dead" Sea.

## Q What was the political landscape like during Joseph's time?

A Joseph's birthplace, in what is now Israel, was a showcase for Roman progress and innovation, with many majestic and beautiful buildings. However, his people had lived under servitude to Rome since 63 BC, with little possibility of advancing. Herod was the local commander, appointed by the Roman Empire in 46 BC. Although he was an able administrator and astute politician, he cruelly killed anyone who opposed his power.

The strange customs of the Romans were at odds with the aspirations of Joseph's people. Their long history was marked by conflicts, victories, defeats, deportations, exiles, monarchies, and unfaithfulness to God. Faith in God was always present, although it was frequently contaminated by idolatry. There was an enormous desire for liberation from foreign domination.

## $Q$  What other issues impacted his society?

$A$  Since the Hebrews were under Roman domination, the majority were poor, except for a small minority who belonged to the privileged class. Their poverty was further compounded by the high tax burden imposed by the Roman Empire on each citizen. The dominant class cruelly exploited a people already suffering crushing poverty. The poor, unproductive soil, scarcity of rain, and primitive agricultural methods made it harder to produce crops, so it was not easy for Joseph's people to sustain themselves.

## $Q$  What were the religious practices like in the time of Joseph?

$A$  The entire religious life, as well as the political and social life of the Jewish people, revolved around the Temple in Jerusalem. King Solomon had built this impressive structure more than 1,000 years before Joseph was born. Nebuchadnezzar destroyed it, and Zerubbabel rebuilt it by 515 BC. Around the time of Joseph's birth, Herod again destroyed the Temple so that he could replace it with an even more exquisite and imposing one, which was completed by AD 64.

The Temple was the place where the Jews prayed and offered sacrifices and burnt offerings. Because of its importance and the constant flow of people attending it, the Temple employed more than 20,000 people to maintain its activities. Their employees ranged from the highest priestly rank to the humblest laborer. Each Hebrew was taxed ten percent of whatever he produced in order to support all that happened at the Temple.

Another important factor in Jewish religious life was the division of the people into groups or classes. The Sadducees were a privileged group, formed from the richest and most influential people, who usually served as the Temple administrators. The Pharisees came next and were characterized by their religious display and practices of prayer, purifications, rules of conduct, and strict observance of the law. The Zealots were a warlike group of revolutionaries, while the

Essenes lived an austere life of self-denial in monastic communities bordering the Dead Sea. Finally, the Samarians were declared heretical and impure pagans who dared to construct their own temple on Mount Gerizim. The region of Samaria was also considered to be cursed land because of a centuries-old division among the Hebrews.

## Q Did men and women share equal status in Joseph's culture?

A No. Women were considered inferior to men and enjoyed no real social standing. Their role was to cook, wash clothes, fetch water, and dedicate themselves to cleaning. They did not participate in functions at the synagogues, and they took their place behind the men when they went to the Temple. They were not permitted to read the Torah in the Temple, a woman's testimony could never be taken into consideration, and no reputable man could ever compliment a woman in public.

## Q What was Joseph's life like at home?

A Joseph probably lived in a modest house, simply constructed of limestone and sun-baked bricks. His main food would have been bread and fish from the Sea of Galilee, not far from his Nazareth home, and he most likely ate locally grown fruits, such as pomegranates, figs, and dates. Meat was very rare in the homes of those with less means, so he probably did not eat meat, but there most likely was olive oil or milk and even wine.

## Q What can we learn from the Holy Family's simple life?

A In the simplicity of his life, Joseph found the profound. In the ordinary events of life in Nazareth, he found the mystery of God. Joseph had less distraction, so he was free to fully love Jesus and Mary, support his family, study Scripture, and to worship and obey God.

## $Q$ Can Joseph help me live like he did?

$A$ Joseph is one of the all-time great examples of obedience. Just think about how he responded when he was told to leave immediately for Egypt: He went! He didn't complain or drag his feet. He responded to God's will and obeyed.

Some say that obediently serving someone, even God, detracts from our freedom. Actually, it's just the opposite. Serving God is an expression of our free will, something we freely choose to do, because there's no greater peace or fulfillment in life than serving God through prayer, worship, and in our relationships with others.

The more obedient we become to God's will, the more we want to grow in this key virtue that Joseph modeled so beautifully.

# Life Links

## Examine

Consider your life and think about it in comparison to Joseph's life. Nothing was more important to Joseph than following the will of God, living a devout life, and serving the interests of Jesus and Mary. How about you?

## Connect

Choose one area of your life that you would like to offer more completely to God. Ask for Joseph to pray for God's help so that you'll be able to change, grow, and live in a way that mirrors the life of Joseph. Take some time to think about Joseph each day and do what you can to live a life committed to God, as he did.

## Transform

If you're willing to grow to be a better person, then place yourself under the protective care of Saint Joseph and seek his fatherly love, protection, and guidance, which is what he offered to the Child Jesus. His powerful intercession can be of great help as you seek to be a light to the world and an image of Christ to others.

CHAPTER TWO

# Joseph in the Bible and Other Early Writings

**Q** **What does the Bible say about Joseph in the Bible?**

**A** The Gospel of John makes only two references to Joseph, but the evangelists Matthew and Luke provide information on Joseph in their detailed descriptions of Jesus' heritage, conception, birth, infancy, and adolescence. He is mentioned by name in seven verses of Matthew, five of Luke, and two of John. Interestingly, no spoken word of Joseph's is recorded in Scripture, except that we know he named the Child "Jesus." Here are some of the facts about Joseph in the Bible:

+ Descendant of the house of David
  (Matthew 1:16, 20; Luke 1:27; 2:4).
+ Husband of Mary (Matthew 1:16–24; Luke 1:27; 2:5).
+ Commonly known as Jesus' father (Matthew 13:55; Luke 2:27, 33, 41, 43, 48; 3:23; 4:22; John 1:45; 6:42).

✦ In a dilemma when faced with the Incarnation of Jesus in Mary's womb (Matthew 1:19).

✦ Went with Mary to Bethlehem for the census ordered by Caesar Augustus (Luke 2:1–4).

✦ Named the Child "Jesus" and fulfilled the Temple rites (Matthew 1:25; Luke 2:21–24, 39).

✦ Fled to Egypt with Mary and Jesus (Matthew 2:13–15).

✦ With Mary, found twelve-year-old Jesus at the Temple in Jerusalem, who returned with them to Nazareth and was subject to them (Luke 2:41–52).

✦ Returned to his hometown of Nazareth (Matthew 2:19–23; Luke 2:39, 51).

✦ Known as the carpenter (Matthew 13:55).
(See "The Complete Gospel Record of Joseph," page 99.)

### Q Why do the Gospels say so little about Joseph?

A The goal of the Gospel writers was to narrate Jesus' life and ministry. Fortunately, Joseph's example of holiness speaks as loudly as any words that could have been used to describe him.

### Q Why are there different names for Joseph's father in the Gospels?

A Two main theories attempt to explain why Joseph's father is listed as Jacob in Matthew's Gospel and Heli in Luke's Gospel:

1. Under the Levirate Law in Deuteronomy (25:5–10), if a married man dies without children, his brother should marry his wife. Their first child would be considered the legal child of her first husband and the natural child of her second husband. If Joseph were such a child, Jacob might be his legal father, whose genealogy is given by Matthew (1:1–17), and Heli would be his natural father, traced by Luke (3:23–38).

2. If Mary were Heli's only child, when Joseph married her he would have the full rights of a son in the family of his father-in-law, so Heli could also be considered his father.

Neither theory is compelling, however, and it must be realized that such detail was not necessary for the evangelists' purposes. Matthew allowed a certain artificiality to show that Jesus was the Messiah legally descended as promised from the line of David, fulfilling the covenant made with Abraham. Luke is more interested in Jesus' relation with all humanity, tracing his lineage all the way back to Adam, for an audience less Jewish than that of Matthew. Both genealogies agree that Joseph is the genealogical—though not biological—father of Jesus, and convey Davidic descent upon him.

### $Q$ Are there any other sources of information about Joseph besides the Bible?

$A$ Yes. Tradition and history offer more information. Please note, however, that the apocryphal or nonauthorized Church writings that date back to early centuries were not believed to be inspired, are unreliable, and are not considered official Church teaching.

### $Q$ What do the apocryphal writings say about Joseph?

$A$ The apocrypha aren't recognized as authentic historical sources and should be thought of as a collection of simple legends and stories. However, for many centuries, these writings influenced popular prayer, devotion, and artistic expression, all of which gave Joseph a particular image as an old man with a white beard when he married Mary. Those who study Saint Joseph have discovered that this was most likely not true.

Another previously believed story says Joseph had married a woman named Melcha, with whom he lived for forty-nine years before marrying Mary. The story says he had four children with

Melcha and was eventually widowed at the age of eighty-nine. Still another story about his marriage to Mary says that she had many suitors wishing to be her husband, and that the high priest allowed her to identify God's choice for a husband from a collection of staffs bearing the name of each man. It was said that she ultimately choose Joseph's staff when it miraculously blossomed. That's one of the reasons why Joseph is often represented in art with a flowering staff as a symbol of his divine election. The lily has also been thought to represent his purity.

### $Q$ Do the writings of the early Church Fathers mention Joseph?

$A$ Yes. Saint Ambrose (d. 397) wrote that Mary and Joseph had a true marriage. Saint Jerome (d. 420) believed that Joseph remained a virgin in marriage. Saint Augustine (d. 430) believed this as well and also defended Joseph's true fatherhood. Many other theologians and Fathers of the Church also supported similar references to Joseph.

### $Q$ How does Joseph's prayer life help my prayer life?

$A$ The stories of Joseph from the Bible tell of a man who was deeply committed to prayer. He knew how to speak to God and, perhaps more importantly, how to listen to God. Joseph can serve as a great model for responding to God's call and living a rewarding life of prayer.

How do we "listen" to God? One way is through silent prayer. Sometimes silence is the most powerful kind of prayer. Words can be distracting, but silence can force us to listen. In silence, we can experience the presence of God in our minds and hearts in a way that we might miss when we're doing all the talking.

Of course, silence can be hard to come by in today's world, where distractions like entertainment, gossip, temptation, and consumerism constantly fight for our attention. It's hard to hear God's voice amid the noise of our culture. To pray effectively, we need to tune out the racket so we can hear the clear message of God and speak with him in the silence of our hearts.

We also need to pray regularly and spend quality time in prayer, daily if we can, or even for just a few seconds before each meal. It could be the first thing you do each morning to prepare yourself for the day ahead, or the last thing you do each evening to reflect on the day gone by. Sometimes making a "prayer appointment" on your daily planner can help make sure time is set aside. The most important thing is to grow in relationship with God. Praying regularly and consistently can help that happen.

## $Q$  What does Joseph's faithfulness mean for me?

$A$  God and Joseph enjoyed a cooperative relationship. Joseph never wavered in his beliefs or commitment to God, and God was faithful to Joseph, giving him the grace and blessings he needed to fulfill his unique role of raising the Son of God.

## Life Links

### Examine

What do you read on a daily basis? Newspapers, Web sites, magazines, novels? What do you read for spiritual nourishment? Are the holy Scriptures included in your daily diet of reading materials, or is your main encounter with God's word during the readings at Sunday Mass? Do you read any other spiritual materials beyond the Bible? Would you like to?

### Connect

Just as Joseph was closely connected to the Word-made-flesh, Jesus, we can connect to him through the Bible—especially in the Gospels of Matthew, Mark, Luke, and John. Think of the Bible as a divine pipeline that can link you directly to his presence in every moment of your earthly life. Now plug in!

### Transform

Daily Scripture reading and regular use of good spiritual books can create momentum in transforming our lives. Commit to taking time each day to read, absorb, and apply what you learn, then see what real change comes about as you grow in God's word.

# CHAPTER THREE

# The Personal Qualities of Joseph

**Q** How is Joseph's holiness expressed?

**A** Joseph's holiness is shown in his unique and intimate union with Mary and Jesus. Their relationship became a constant response of love for God, expressed in simple and generous acceptance of his will. Joseph's holiness is also expressed in the title given him in Matthew 1:19: "a just man," meaning a man whom Father Jean-Jacques Olier, founder of the Society of Saint-Sulpice, describes as "thus able to make visible the admirable perfection of God the Father."

**Q** What are the most important virtues Joseph possessed?

**A** The main virtues espoused by the Church are faith, hope, and love. We can only imagine how Joseph embodied these virtues, but the fruits of his life certainly gave witness to all three.

**Faith:** Joseph showed tremendous faith when he was asked to be husband to a virgin and father to her unborn child, even though a virginal conception was a mystery beyond comprehension. Faith is clearly the foundation of the holiness of Joseph, the just man, as in Romans 1:17, where we learn that "the just man lives by faith."

**Hope:** Joseph remained calm and full of positive hope while in Bethlehem, as Mary was about to give birth amid very difficult circumstances. He also demonstrated hope when he had to flee into Egypt and live there for several years, and when he searched diligently for twelve-year-old Jesus in Jerusalem. He maintained belief in God throughout all these struggles.

**Love:** Joseph loved Mary and Jesus in the fullest, most complete way possible. He trusted in God's plan for all their lives, and in that trust offered his total love of God, God's Son, and his wife, Mary.

Joseph also displayed the moral or cardinal virtues of: *prudence* in faithfully guarding the secret of the Incarnation; *justice*, as he placed complete trust in Mary and Jesus and provided for them; *fortitude* to courageously overcome all the difficulties that confronted him; and *temperance*, as he lived his life as a humble carpenter in Nazareth.

## Q How did Joseph display his dignity?

*A* We can see tremendous dignity in Joseph's role as father to Jesus, who was obedient and subject to him while Joseph loved, educated, and accompanied him every day. Through his fatherhood of Jesus, Joseph not only fulfilled the unique role God created for him, he also cooperated in the mystery of our own redemption as he guided God's Son as he grew in faith and wisdom.

## Q How does Joseph play a part in our redemption?

A As Mary's husband and Jesus' earthly father, Joseph was actively involved in the mystery of Jesus' Incarnation. In fact, his role was second only to Mary's. Although Joseph did not participate directly in Jesus' conception, Joseph acted as his father by supporting, protecting, educating him, and sharing a good portion of his life with him. By being an integral part of Jesus' life, Joseph, like Mary, helped form Jesus for his mission of redemption.

## Q Was Joseph sanctified before birth, since he was called "a just man?"

A In the New Testament, the word "just" or "righteous" is usually reserved for God, which indicates how much the Gospel writer esteems Joseph. Naturally, this has led many to praise Joseph's great sanctity, and rightfully so. But some, such as scholars Jean Gerson and Bernardino de Bustis, went so far as to say he was sanctified in his mother's womb—a privilege also accorded to Jeremiah ("Before I formed you in the womb...I consecrated you" [Jeremiah 1:5]) and John the Baptist ("He will be filled with the Holy Spirit, even from his mother's womb" [Luke 1:15]). Still other thinkers, such as Alexis-Henri-Marie Cardinal Lépicier, believed Joseph lived his entire life without any personal sin. While it's interesting to consider these opinions, it's important to understand that they are merely speculation and have never been officially taught by the Church.

## Q Is silence one of Joseph's virtues, since his words are not quoted in Scripture?

A Yes. In fact, Joseph's silence is so striking that the Gospels seem to present it as his personal trademark. When the angel commanded him to take Mary as his wife, he obeyed simply in silence to fulfill God's will. When Jesus was born and later presented in the Temple, not a single word of Joseph's is recorded. While both Mary and

Joseph were present when Jesus was found in the Temple courtyard in Jerusalem, only Mary is quoted in Scripture.

Joseph's silence can be seen as an extension of his humility. Joseph was destined by God, as Paul VI said, "to be as an obscure shadow near Jesus, more to conceal the rays of that divine sun than to be illuminated by it, more to absorb the rays than to reflect them."

## Q  Do we know if Joseph was a patient man?

A  Patience is the virtue that helps us endure in the face of trials and troubles. Patience requires self-control. We can only imagine the extent of Joseph's patience, but his life with Mary and Jesus shows us that he trusted in God as he walked into the unknown, took Mary as his wife, and cared for her and Jesus amid persecution and other hardships.

## Q  What can Joseph teach us about humility?

A  Joseph was chosen for the amazing responsibility of raising God's Son and yet was humble as he surrendered himself to God's will, despite the mystery that surrounded Mary giving birth while still a virgin and all that followed in their life together as a family. In his humility, Joseph shows us tremendous power, strength, and virtue.

## Q  Did Joseph ever laugh?

A  We can only speculate, but it makes sense that Joseph would have a sense of humor. As a man of the people and a craftsman, Joseph would have seen the human events that occur in everyday living, and it's easy to see him sharing stories and laughing with his family and friends.

There are times when we may find it hard to see the humor in life. Joseph can help us accept—and even laugh at—our imperfect world. It certainly wasn't a perfect world for him—far from it—yet he likely found a way to focus on God's goodness.

*Q* **How do Joseph's qualities help us on our path to holiness?**

*A* From Joseph, we learn that we can live our ordinary lives in an extraordinary way by practicing the virtues he models. His spirituality is composed of simple acts, making him a model for people of every vocation. He teaches us, in the words of Pope Paul VI, that, "in order to be a good and genuine follower of Christ, there is no need of great things—it is enough to have the common, simple, and human virtues, but they need to be true and authentic."

## Life Links

### Examine
Take a look at where your life is right now. How would you like Joseph's help? How can the virtues that Joseph modeled support you in your daily living?

### Connect
Asking Joseph to pray for your needs requires entrusting him with your life. Put your cares in his strong, fatherly hands and seek his intercession for the virtues you need most. Pray daily for Joseph's protection and care.

### Transform
If you truly want to change, it is important to look at what you need to do each day to make that happen. Seek virtues to grow in holiness and root out all that prevents you from being the person you believe God is calling you to be. Look to Saint Joseph as a powerful ally along the way.

CHAPTER FOUR

# Joseph's Life as Husband to Mary

**Q** How do we know Joseph was Mary's husband?

**A** We know it in the same way we learn about most of Jesus' life: through the Bible. The evangelists Luke and Matthew (Luke 2:4–5; Matthew 1:16, 19–20, 24) name Joseph as Mary's husband and tell us that Joseph took his wife and led her into his house, where they lived with Jesus.

**Q** What can Joseph teach us about marriage?

**A** Joseph is the very model of a man of God: a husband and father, giving his entire self to Mary and Jesus. He was married to the most grace-filled woman God could provide as mother for his Son, and certainly he must have shared in her deep interior life and holiness.

Through his daily companionship with Mary, Joseph no doubt grew in holiness. Today, Joseph and Mary show couples how to grow in personal holiness and strengthen their marriage bond. Together, husbands and wives can create a home environment that enables their love to be modeled for their children, as husbands are "Joseph" to their wives, and wives are "Mary" to their husbands.

## Q How did Joseph and Mary discover their vocation to marriage?

A Joseph and Mary's call to marriage was probably more powerful than that of any other couple in history. Joseph and Mary were called by God himself to collaborate in the mystery of the Incarnation of Jesus, who was to be born of a woman who was married yet was also a virgin. He was to be born into a family: the cornerstone of civilization and the model of God's love. To create that family, it was necessary for Joseph and Mary to be married so that the coming of God's Son would be within the context of matrimony.

God gave Joseph and Mary every opportunity to build the deep, mutual love that leads to the rich communion of life enjoyed by a man and woman in marriage. So when Joseph and Mary came together to discover this vocation, it wasn't just a coincidence—it was the direct result of God's loving intervention.

## Q Were marriages celebrated in Joseph's time in the same way we celebrate them today?

A No, the customs then were quite different from today's marriage ceremonies. At that time, marriages took place in two stages: the betrothal and, months later, the actual celebration of the groom taking the bride into his home. The betrothal ceremony was very simple and usually took place in the home of the bride's father, where the groom would pay his new father-in-law a dowry in exchange for the father's "gift" of his daughter. At that moment, the woman belonged to her husband by right and by law, even though she would continue to live in her father's house. The marriage was already sealed and official, and the man and woman were considered espoused. If the bride was unfaithful during this time, she was treated as an adulteress and subject to legal punishment, including stoning.

## Q  How was the second stage of marriage celebrated?

A  This was a solemn celebration, even more so than today's wedding ceremonies. It would take place at night, and the bride would be dressed up with her head crowned with flowers, waiting with her maiden friends in her father's house for the groom to arrive with his groomsmen. The ceremony would take place in the presence of the guests, with the groom telling the bride, "You are my wife, and I am your husband today and forever." The couple and their guests would then begin a feast that could last up to a week.

## Q  At what stage did the angel tell Mary she would give birth to Jesus?

A  Some believe the angel's annunciation took place after the second stage of marriage, when Joseph had already taken Mary into his home, although the couple had no sexual relations. They believe that when the angel later told Joseph to take Mary as his wife, he was simply instructing Joseph to remain as he was with her.

More commonly, it is thought that the annunciation took place after the first stage but before the second stage of marriage, "When his mother Mary had been betrothed to Joseph, before they came together she was found to be with child of the Holy Spirit" (Matthew 1:18, consistent also with Luke 1:27, 34). When the angel tells Joseph "[D]o not fear to take Mary your wife," he is telling him to proceed to the second stage and take her into his home as planned. Remember, during the first stage (betrothal) the bride and groom were already referred to as husband and wife. In fact, to break betrothal was considered divorce.

**Q** **Why does Matthew specify that Mary became pregnant by the Holy Spirit before she lived together with Joseph?**

**A** He is making it clear that Mary was a virgin when Jesus was conceived, and he is excluding the involvement of any man. Matthew is also careful to declare that Mary and "Joseph her husband" were already considered married when the virginal conception took place.

**Q** **Did Joseph know that Mary was pregnant with the Messiah?**

**A** Based on Matthew 1:18–19, some theologians believe Mary kept silent about the angel's annunciation and that Joseph was completely unaware of the significance of the baby Mary carried. But others note that it wouldn't seem right for Mary to withhold such news from Joseph, since God's work was being entrusted to both of them. So it's probable that Mary would have confided in Joseph and that he would have known exactly what had occurred in Mary.

**Q** **If Joseph was a "just man," then why did he think about leaving Mary?**

**A** Joseph is not called "just" for his observance of the Mosaic law authorizing the husband to divorce his wife in case of adultery, which doesn't apply to Mary. Nor is he "just" for wanting to be fair to his innocent wife who had not committed adultery. His motive was not that he suspected Mary of unfaithfulness and thought he would kindly leave her so as not to shame her. Nor was it his confusion at not being able to explain the fact of her pregnancy. Rather, on realizing the great mission that God had entrusted to his wife, as Mother of the Messiah, he found himself in the presence of that mysterious divine plan, before which the just man had to consider stepping aside. He is "just" because he believed in God's promise and humbly recognized his unworthiness to presume to act as father to the divine Child.

## $Q$  But why would he leave a pregnant wife?

$A$  Joseph's humble response is just as understandable as that of any other heroes of the faith when God was about to break into their history or anyone else awaiting the arrival of the Messiah. Moses removed his sandals in unworthiness before the burning bush (Exodus 3:5). Isaiah was utterly overwhelmed by the vision of God (Isaiah 6:5). Elizabeth wondered how it was possible that the mother of the Savior could come to her (Luke 1:43). And Peter exclaimed to Jesus, "Depart from me, for I am a sinful man, O Lord" (Luke 5:8).

## $Q$  What do we know about Joseph's virginity?

$A$  Saint Thomas Aquinas gives us two good reasons for believing in Joseph's virginity, "...because we see nowhere that he had another wife and because a saint does not succumb to fornication." Plus, since virginity is a gift of God (1 Corinthians 7:32), it makes sense that God would give Joseph this gift in light of his special mission. God chose Joseph as husband to the Virgin Mary, calling him to live his virginity at Mary's side, fully aware of his wife's mission. By God's design, Joseph and Mary shared a special marital love that was also virginal.

## $Q$  If Mary and Joseph lived in virginity, did they have a true marriage?

$A$  Joseph is truly Mary's husband by virtue of their betrothal and marriage, but there were no sexual relations between them. Matthew calls Joseph Mary's husband, (1:16, 19). It is clear that though they did not share sexual relations, they shared the special and intimate love that makes a marriage. Saint Augustine emphasized that all the essential elements of a true marriage are present: offspring, being the Lord Jesus himself; fidelity, since there was no adultery; and the sacrament, since there was no divorce, which under Mosaic law dissolved a marriage.

## Q What kind of marriage did Joseph and Mary share?

A Mary's marriage to Joseph was ordained by God to receive and raise Jesus. Therefore, it required the greatest expression of conjugal union, that is, the total and complete giving of each one to the other. Bernardino de Bustis tells us that there existed a most holy and indivisible love between Mary and Joseph. As husband, Joseph, therefore, lived a profound experience of the intimate bond of communion with Mary. He shared daily life with her and loved her intensely. In the same way, with the natural feeling of a wife, Mary cultivated in her heart sentiments and affections destined exclusively for Joseph.

# Life Links

## Examine

If you're in a married state of life, make a daily, focused effort to love your spouse in a very special way. How? By doing everything you can to help your spouse get to heaven! What better demonstration of your love than desiring to spend eternity with your spouse in the presence of God?

If you're single yet called to the vocation of marriage, think about the qualities you envision in your future spouse. Are you focused on superficial qualities like appearance and wealth, or do you look at deeper qualities like your future spouse's closeness to God and the devout practice of his or her faith?

If you're called to the special vocation of consecrated virginity, imitate Joseph's deep faith in God and pure love for Mary. Regardless of your state of life, consider Joseph's devotion to Mary. It's a powerful mirror for measuring your devotion to supporting and caring for the ones you love.

## Connect

Connecting with the essence of Joseph's deep and profound love for Mary can help inspire and encourage your connection with others. As Joseph served the interests of his wife, you can serve the interests of your family, your friends—even the strangers you encounter in your daily life.

## Transform

The effort you make to help others grow closer to God allows you to become more and more like the person God wants you to become.

# CHAPTER FIVE

# Joseph's Life as Father to Jesus

**Q** **Why was Jesus born in Bethlehem instead of Nazareth, where Joseph and Mary lived?**

**A** In the Gospel of Luke (2:1–12), we learn that Emperor Caesar Augustus ordered a census that required all citizens to return to their family's native town in order to be registered. Since Joseph was a descendant of David, he needed to leave Nazareth and go to the city of David (Bethlehem) along with his wife, Mary, who was pregnant. This resulted in Jesus being born in Bethlehem instead of Nazareth. By his order, the emperor unwittingly contributed to the fulfillment of prophecy, which specified the Messiah would come from Bethlehem (Micah 5:1–3; Matthew 2:5) and that he would be a descendant of David (2 Samuel 7:12–14; Matthew 1:20). It was through Joseph, "son of David" (Matthew 1:20), that the Davidic genealogy was transmitted to Jesus so that he was, indeed, held to be a descendant of David.

## Q How did Jesus' circumcision take place?

A Circumcision, a sign of the Hebrews' pact with God and the holiness of Israel among all the nations, was required by Jewish law. Since it enabled a child to become a member of the covenant people, circumcision was very important for Jewish families and was celebrated solemnly.

Traditionally, one of a man's first duties as father was to circumcise his son in fulfillment of the law. The mother could also do it (Exodus 4:25). Joseph fulfilled the rite for Jesus in the presence of witnesses, as required by Talmudic tradition. By accepting this obligation, Joseph became a "minister of circumcision" for the Child, reciting the words, "Blessed be the Lord, our God, who sanctified us with his precepts and permitted us to introduce our son into the covenant of Abraham, our father." Of course, Jesus brought the Old Covenant to fulfillment and established the New Covenant in his Blood.

## Q Who gave the name "Jesus" to God's Son?

A While the angel first told Mary that she would call the child's name Jesus (Luke 1:31), it was Joseph who was given the fatherly mission of actually conferring the name, "...you shall call his name Jesus, for he will save his people from their sins" (Matthew 1:21).

Joseph fulfilled this function at the circumcision when Jesus was eight days old (Luke 2:21), a tradition that underscored a father's authority over his son. When he gave the name to the Child (Matthew 1:25), Joseph acted as God's representative, fulfilling all the rights and duties of the father of Jesus. Pope Pius XII described Joseph's role in relation to Jesus by saying that he had for Jesus, "by a special gift from heaven, all the natural love, all the affectionate care that a father's heart could know."

## $Q$  What was Joseph's role in the presentation of Jesus in the Temple?

$A$  Under Jewish law, every firstborn child was to be consecrated to God (Exodus 13:1–15). Joseph had an important role in this rite, since one of a father's duties was to redeem his firstborn son before God by offering five silver pieces to the Temple treasury. The law also decreed that a mother needed to be purified on the fortieth day after giving birth (Leviticus 12). While these were two separate and unique rites, Luke freely mixed their details in his Gospel as he describes Joseph's offering of two doves or pigeons, the poorer of the two options prescribed for the purification (Leviticus 12:6). As a result, by exercising his fatherhood for Jesus by making the offering for the firstborn, Joseph again acted as a "minister of salvation." All of this was in careful obedience "to the law of the Lord" (Luke 2:23, 24, 39).

## $Q$  What is the significance of the Holy Family's flight into Egypt?

$A$  In Matthew's Gospel (2:13–22), we see Joseph exercising his rights and duties as head of the Holy Family. The angel appears to him and tells him where he must flee with Mary and Jesus, and Joseph obeys immediately.

But the Holy Family's escape to and return from Egypt is significant for other reasons as well. It fulfills the prophecy of Hosea (11:1), "Out of Egypt I have called my Son" (Matthew 2:15). And it symbolizes true liberation, which the children of Israel experienced in the ancient exodus. Here, Jesus is seen as the true Moses who leads his people toward ultimate liberation. Pope John Paul II writes, "Just as Israel had followed the path of the exodus 'from the condition of slavery' in order to begin the Old Covenant, so Joseph, guardian and cooperator in the providential mystery of God, even in exile, watched over the one who brings about the New Covenant" (the apostolic exhortation on Saint Joseph, *Redemptoris Custos* [RC], 14).

By saving Jesus' life from the threat of death, Joseph once more acts as a "minister of salvation," since at that critical moment all salvation was placed in his hands. This event illustrates the human weakness that the Son of God took on in becoming incarnate, totally entrusting himself into the hands of Joseph while giving up any kind of miraculous intervention.

### Q  How did the Holy Family live in Egypt?

A  Matthew doesn't give much information about this event, saying only, "Joseph rose and took the child and his mother by night, and departed to Egypt" (2:14). So Joseph could have merely crossed the border into Egypt south of Gaza, outside of Herod's dominion, or he could have gone to any of the various places in Egypt that claim to have hosted the Holy Family. What's important for us to know is that God chose a safe place for Joseph and his family, most likely in one of the Jewish settlements near the border, where he could easily find work and support his family.

Since Saint Joseph most probably lived amid his compatriots in Egypt, he would not have encountered much difficulty in finding work and getting established there. This is especially so since the Jewish colonies in Egypt formed a structured association of reciprocal collaboration among themselves.

### Q  How long did the Holy Family live in Egypt?

A  Some historians believe Herod died two years after the slaughter of the holy innocents, which Jesus had escaped by fleeing into Egypt. The angel then ordered Joseph to return: "'Rise, take the child and his mother and go to the land of Israel...' ...And being warned in a dream he withdrew to the district of Galilee. And he went and dwelt in a city called Nazareth" (Matthew 2:20–23). So the length of their stay in Egypt could have been about two years, after which Joseph returned to his ordinary life with Jesus and Mary, working as a carpenter in Nazareth.

### Q What's the significance of Jesus being lost when he was twelve?

*A* Turning twelve was a very important occasion in Jewish culture, marking passage from childhood to adulthood. So when Jesus went with his parents to participate in the paschal feast in Jerusalem, it would have been his first official opportunity to take part in worship in the Temple. The huge number of pilgrims arriving in Jerusalem for this occasion could have caused its population to swell to 150,000—significantly larger than the little town of Nazareth, and a very different world for Jesus and his parents.

When Jesus became "lost," it wasn't the result of his parents' carelessness, but rather Jesus' own decision to remain behind in the Temple precincts of the city to hear and question the rabbis. It was perhaps a sign that this was no ordinary twelve-year-old.

### Q What happened after Jesus was found in the Temple?

*A* Luke tells us that Jesus "went down with them [Joseph and Mary] and came to Nazareth, and was obedient to them....And Jesus increased in wisdom and in stature, and in favor with God and man" (2:51–52). Living with Joseph and Mary in Nazareth, Jesus humbly obeyed his parents and learned from them as he prepared to fulfill his messianic mission. As he grew, Jesus obeyed and worked together with Joseph and Mary, dedicated to the duties he performed with his family and the work he did with his father. We aren't given details about this stage of Jesus' life, but we can be sure that it was marked by the continual, loving presence of Joseph, his father and educator.

### Q How can the father-son relationship between Joseph and Jesus apply to my life?

*A* Everything Joseph did was in service to the Son of God. Just as Joseph taught young Jesus about the tools of a craftsman, we are called to teach our children about the tools for faith and life.

## Q  What was life like for the Holy Family in Nazareth?

A  Nazareth was a small, insignificant working-class town at the time of Joseph, who would have worked hard with his skilled hands to earn a living for his family. Young Jesus witnessed this model of fatherly love, as well as Mary's example of blessing daily family life. The Holy Family lived an ordinary life in the sight of others, while Jesus "grew and became strong, filled with wisdom" (Luke 2:40).

Like any other child, Jesus would have grown to know his surroundings and learn the art of carpentry from Joseph. He would have attended the synagogue and listened to the sacred word while, under his parents' instruction, learning his people's history and becoming familiar with their sacred texts.

## Q  How did Joseph fulfill his role as father of Jesus?

A  Joseph fulfilled his fatherly role by living with Jesus, embracing him, raising, and educating him with love and affection. As Pope Pius XII said, Joseph had toward Jesus "all the natural love, all the affectionate solicitude that a father's heart can know" (radio message, February 19, 1958).

Joseph lived his life totally at the service of Jesus and was always aware of his special mission. In the words of Paul VI, Saint Joseph decided "to put his liberty at once at the disposition of the divine designs, along with his legitimate human calling, his conjugal happiness; to accept the conditions, the responsibility, and the burden of a family, but, through an incomparable virginal love, to renounce that natural conjugal love that is the foundation and the nourishment of the family. In this way he offered the whole of his existence in a total sacrifice to the imponderable demands raised by the astonishing coming of the Messiah" (homily, March 27, 1969).

## $Q$  Did Joseph love Jesus as fully as he would a biological son?

$A$  Joseph was chosen for the incredible purpose of being God's representative in the raising of his Son, so he must certainly have demonstrated complete fatherly love and authority according to God's own heart. Joseph's love would have been unlimited, shown in generosity, sacrifice, and unconditional service to Jesus, just as if he were his own biological son. If Joseph's love had been any less, God would certainly not have entrusted him with this most precious mystery.

## $Q$  How can we say that Joseph is Jesus' father, rather than simply his guardian?

$A$  First of all, the evangelists clearly say that Joseph is Jesus' "father" (Luke 2:27, 33, 41, 43, 48; 3:23; Matthew 13:55). This alone is enough to make him truly a father in the full sense of the word. Joseph's paternity is not biological or genetic, but it is the human, legal, affectionate fatherhood needed to raise young Jesus.

Being a father involves much more than a physical function. Saint Thomas said, "Joseph is understood to be Jesus' father in the same way that he is Mary's husband, not by carnal union, but by the bond of the marriage itself." Joseph was obedient to his call to fatherhood before Jesus was born, making his relationship with Jesus much deeper than that for a son adopted into a marriage after conception and birth.

Origen observed that the title "father" didn't lose its meaning when it was bestowed on Joseph by the work of the Holy Spirit. Rather, just as Mary received a mother's heart, the Holy Spirit formed a father's heart in Joseph.

## Q  What word best describes Joseph's fatherhood?

*A* Some people call him Jesus' "*adoptive* father," even though the term is inadequate. "Adoptive" indicates a relationship that is established legally after birth, rather than being based on family ties. Jesus was certainly not alien to his family and, by God's plan, Joseph's fatherhood was personal.

Others call him Jesus' "*legal* father," based on the angel telling Joseph to take Mary, his wife, and to be the one to name the Child Jesus (Matthew 1:21). This term is accurate, but only in a juridical or law-based understanding. "Legal" conveys that Jesus is recognized by the law as Joseph's son—a truth vital to establishing Jesus as Messiah, through the lineage of David through Joseph. On the other hand, the term fails to capture the intimate relationship between father and child.

Many theologians prefer to call Joseph Jesus' "*virginal* father." This term has the advantage of describing the unique nature of this fatherhood and the virginal marriage into which Jesus was born. But it also has the disadvantage of being confused with the virginal motherhood of Mary, as Joseph had no physical part in Jesus' conception.

Another common term is "*foster* father," which implies Joseph's dedication as a parent, as well as his role of nourishing, defending, and caring for Jesus. But because "foster" is essentially limited to these roles, its definition is too narrow to capture the full essence of Joseph's fatherhood.

The term "*chosen* father" conveys the important truth that Joseph's fatherhood is established as a vocation divinely given. However, natural fathers and even adoptive or foster fathers may consider their fatherly role as chosen for them by God.

Some Joseph scholars suggest the title "*matrimonial* father," since it is Joseph's marriage to Mary that fulfills God's purpose for receiving Jesus. Unfortunately, this word isn't widely used in everyday conversation, so it is difficult for many to grasp its meaning, as is also true for the term *"vicar* father," which implies that Joseph is acting in the place of God the Father.

Finally, some use the name *"putative"* or *"presumed* father," based on Luke 3:23, "Jesus was about thirty years of age, being the son (as was supposed) of Joseph." These terms indicate that the inhabitants of Nazareth considered him Jesus' father, but they give no insight into the true nature of that fatherhood.

None of these terms totally captures Joseph's special relationship with Jesus and the dignity he shared with Mary, Jesus' mother. Perhaps it is best to simply call Joseph "Jesus' father," just as Scripture itself does (Luke 2:27, 33, 41, 43, 48; Matthew 13:55), without adding any adjective to the title.

## $Q$ How did Joseph fulfill his mission of being Jesus' father?

$A$ The Gospel writers present the following as evidence of Joseph's fatherhood:

+ He was a descendent of David, so that Jesus could be recognized as "Son of David," since Joseph was of the house and family of David (Luke 2:4).

+ He saw to the rite of circumcision (Luke 2:21), by which Jesus took membership in the people of the Covenant.

+ He named the Child (Matthew 1:25), a fatherly right that identifies Jesus as his son.

+ He redeemed the firstborn through the rite of presenting Jesus in the Temple (Luke 2:22ff).

+ He cared for the Child and his mother during the flight and stay in Egypt (Matthew 2:13–22).

+ He lived a life dedicated to family and work, and he had Jesus obey him (Luke 2:51).

## Q How did Joseph educate Jesus?

A In Joseph's time, one of the most important responsibilities for fathers was to educate their sons. However, much of what is learned comes through example, rather than through formal teaching. As Jesus observed Joseph in his everyday life, he experienced an education based on example, harmony, and an eagerness to do God's will in simplicity. Joseph was a model worthy of imitation, inspiring Pope Paul VI to declare, "Saint Joseph is proof that to be good and authentic followers of Christ, great things are not necessary, but what are sufficient and necessary are the common virtues, human and simple, but true and authentic" (allocution of March 19, 1969).

Just as today's children are greatly influenced by the environment in which they're raised, the same was true for Jesus. Pope Paul VI understood this point, observing that the long years Jesus spent with Joseph were reflected in his behavior: "Once Jesus leaves his small workshop in Nazareth and begins his mission as prophet and teacher, Saint Joseph is the image of the Gospel that he proclaims for the redemption of humanity." In other words, Jesus' image of the "new man" (Ephesians 2:15) had been formed during his thirty years of living in the Holy Family, where Joseph was always before his eyes as the model of godly manhood.

## Q What other ways did Joseph help educate Jesus?

A Joseph fulfilled the practical obligations of fathers in his time. This included the religious education of his son. This consisted of teaching passages of sacred Scripture and God's precepts to his people through oral tradition. Readings would be followed by explanations, questions, and answers (Deuteronomy 8:6–20; Exodus 13:8).

Joseph also taught Jesus his own profession of carpentry, which was customarily passed on from father to son (Matthew 13:55; Mark 6:3). The years Jesus spent working with Joseph at the carpenter's bench became a daily expression of love lived in the warmth of his family.

Finally, Joseph gave Jesus a good Jewish education. Jesus would have learned such practices as daily prayers and participation in the local synagogue, but Joseph provided all the practical education of a good Jewish father, and even more so because God gave him the vocation to serve the person and mission of Jesus through his fatherhood.

## $Q$ Why do some people think Joseph and Mary had other children?

$A$ The Church has always taught that Mary remained a virgin and that she and Joseph were celibate in their marriage. A strong tradition also holds that Joseph was a virgin, contrary to the apocryphal or noncanonical writings. The fact that they never had sexual relations in no way diminished their love.

Luke 8:19–20 tells us, "Then [Jesus'] mother and his brothers came to him, but they could not reach him for the crowd. And he was told, 'Your mother and your brothers are standing outside, desiring to see you.'" Some people mistakenly believe the "brothers of Jesus" in this passage were conceived by Mary. The word "brothers," however, had the broader meaning of "relatives" and was even applied to those who enjoyed strong friendship. There is no biblical proof that Mary and Joseph had other children.

In order to defend Mary's virginity, the apocrypha resolved the problem of "Jesus' brothers" by saying that Joseph was already widowed when he married Mary and that he had children by his previous marriage. However, there is no evidence that this was the case.

Matthew 1:24–25 says, "When Joseph woke from sleep, he did as the angel of the Lord commanded him; he took his wife, but knew her not until she had borne a son; and he called his name Jesus." The phrase "knew her not" means that Joseph and Mary had no sexual relations. Some misinterpret the word "until" to imply that they did have such relations after Jesus was born. Again, this belief has no foundation, since the passage is concerned only with describing the virginal conception and birth, and not with whether or not they later had conjugal relations.

Also, when Luke 2:7 says Mary "gave birth to her firstborn son," it does not imply that she had other children after Jesus. The Bible uses the word "firstborn" simply to indicate the one entitled to the privileges specified by the Mosaic laws, such as the special consecration when Jesus is taken to the Temple (Luke 2:22; Exodus 13:2).

## Life Links

### Examine

Consider the men in your life who have been a source of influence and inspiration. Your father? Perhaps an uncle or grandfather? A male mentor or family friend? In a similar but more profound way, Joseph can occupy a prominent place in your life. What would you like to most learn from him?

### Connect

While we all have a biological father and mother, we also have an inherent spiritual father and mother in Joseph and Mary. By embracing them, we can learn what they know so intimately: what it means to live alongside Christ, to share sorrows and joys, to live in complete devotion to the Son of God.

### Transform

You can achieve a fresh outlook on life by seeking to imitate Joseph's fatherly qualities in your manner of relating to others. This will give you a clear path for becoming more and more the person God wants you to be. You can also gain insight into God's will and purpose for your life, as well as an eternal perspective in all that you think, say, and do.

CHAPTER SIX

# Joseph's Life as Worker

**Q** Was Joseph really a carpenter?

**A** We learn of Joseph's profession from Matthew 13:55, usually translated to read that Jesus became known as "the carpenter's son." But Joseph's carpentry probably encompassed more than just home construction. It might be more accurate to call him a craftsman—someone who could be called upon to build basic furnishings, cabinets, tools, and a wide variety of other essential items. Joseph was most likely experienced in it from his youth, as a career handed down by his father and, in turn, handed down to Jesus in keeping with the custom of the time.

The Gospels tell us that Joseph practiced his trade in Nazareth, a small town hidden in the hills near Galilee, a village of laborers, poor and simple people. As a result, Joseph would likely have made simple furnishings, tools, and household items, rather than refined furniture or expensive artistic items for the wealthy.

## Q Did Joseph only work with wood?

**A** The Greek word for Joseph's profession is *tekton*—a "worker of hard materials." So it is likely that Joseph worked with more than just wood and probably worked with heavy wood, stone, and even metal. In his workshop, he would make furniture, doors, windows, and other necessities for local townspeople. Outside his shop, Joseph would likely have been seen repairing a plow or wagon wheel, laying the foundation for a house, or other related manual labor.

## Q Is there a special meaning to Joseph's work?

**A** Yes. Not only did Joseph's work give him the means for supporting his family, but it also became part of Jesus' education. So much so, in fact, that Jesus learned to work with his hands in the same profession and became known as "the carpenter" (Mark 6:3). This didn't happen by accident: Jesus actively chose to be known in this way, linking his social position and earthly identity with Joseph and his work.

## Q How did Joseph's work help form Jesus' identity?

**A** While Joseph's fatherhood transmitted Jesus' royal title of "son of David," Joseph's work gave him the identity "son of the carpenter." Joseph's style of work was so humble and basic that Jesus chose to appropriate it to himself. Pope John Paul II highlighted this dynamic, saying, "At the workbench where he plied his trade together with Jesus, Joseph brought human work closer to the mystery of Redemption" (*RC* 22).

## Q Why is Joseph considered the patron of workers?

**A** Other saints also worked as much as or even more than Joseph did, but his work had a special purpose, which was to raise and educate the Son of God, and also to provide for Mary, his wife.

Jesus learned his profession and livelihood for thirty years from Joseph. "The one who, while *being God, became like us in all things* (see Hebrews 2:17; Philippians 2:5–8) devoted most of the years of his life on earth to *manual work* at the carpenter's bench" (*Laborem Exercens, 6*).

While all popes in recent times have consistently presented Joseph as the model of workers and laborers, Pope Pius XII instituted this liturgical feast on May 1, 1955. He said: "By family ties, daily communion, spiritual harmony, and divine grace, Joseph, of David's line, was more closely bonded to Jesus, than was any other man, and yet he was a humble worker."

## Q  What do we have in common with Joseph's purpose in life?

*A* We are also called to use our God-given skills and virtues to serve Christ in our home, the Church, and the world. This is the unique role God has prepared for us to play in the story of salvation. This is our life's work.

We can think of these skills and virtues as "tools" for completing our mission. We can only speculate on what would have happened if Joseph had said "no" to God, to Mary and, ultimately, to Jesus. Thank God he said "yes" and said it often as God's plan unfolded before him over the course of his life.

## Q  How can Joseph help make my life better?

*A* By challenging us to follow in his footsteps and live a life of simplicity. Joseph always put God first. Everything else was secondary—this can be a simple formula for following God's will without distraction. With his priorities in place, Joseph was able to dedicate himself to God's plan for the well-being, care, and protection of Jesus and Mary.

### Q As patron of workers, how can Joseph help me with my career choice and job?

A Without a doubt, all Christians should look to Saint Joseph as a perfect example of being totally available to God's will and humbly and faithfully fulfilling the divine plan for the Incarnation.

In a word, Joseph is the *model* for every Christian, since he is the Gospel ideal to which Jesus will allude in his preaching. He offers us a compelling example of availability to God's call, of calm in every situation, of total trust founded on a life of supernatural faith and charity, and of great prayer.

Pope John Paul II observed that "work was the daily expression of love in the life of the Family of Nazareth" (*RC 22*). This gives the phrase "labor of love" a whole new meaning, as our jobs provide a way for us to participate in the work of creation and redemption as we seek to answer God's call.

Joseph's work enabled him to fully participate in God's plan. Our work can help us do the same.

### Q What else was Joseph committed to beyond serving God and his family?

A Joseph was also committed to an interior life of prayer and spiritual growth. Joseph exemplifies a spirituality that is accessible to everyone, since it builds on the importance of daily life itself. Each person is to learn to live his or her ordinary life in an extraordinary manner. Joseph's spirituality is built on simple acts. This is why he is the ideal model for priests, religious, parents, spouses, and all classes of people. He teaches us that "in order to be a good and genuine follower of Christ, there is no need of great things—it is enough to have the common, simple and human virtues, but they need to be true and authentic," as Pope Paul VI asserted.

In the end, Joseph's interior life can be summed up in one word: *God*. God is the sole object of his thoughts and desires. The interior life is about the kingdom of God within us, made even more holy by keeping worldly affairs and material acquisitions at bay and focusing instead on our commitment to Christ.

# Life Links

### Examine
Each of us possesses a collection of God-given gifts and talents. How do you use them? Do you try to touch the lives of others in positive ways? Do you see your abilities as ways of honoring God and giving him credit for your achievements? Do you see work as an expression of love for God and others? Without that perspective, it's easy to see work as nothing more than a means of financial reward—an incomplete and shallow definition indeed.

### Connect
Take a moment and try to picture Joseph at work. Visualize a young, robust guy tough enough to tackle large timbers, chunks of stone, implements of metal and more. Now, rather than picture how he worked, picture why: to serve God and support his family. You may not be as strong or rugged as Joseph, but you can work with the same vigor and purpose as he did. He shows us the connection between the role of worker and the role of servant.

### Transform
As patron of workers, Joseph helps those who are out of work, those deciding on an educational or career path, and those in established occupations. He's a model for all forms of work, not just for employees and employers, but also for stay-at-home parents, elderly volunteers, and young children in school. Where there is work to be done, Joseph will protect, equip, and guide us in all of our needs. Go to him.

## CHAPTER SEVEN

# Joseph's Death

**Q** **Why should I care about Joseph's death?**

**A** Joseph had a remarkable interior spirituality—a genuine peace of mind, soul, and heart. He is a model for those who seek the interior life because he "was in daily contact with the mystery 'hidden from ages past,' and which dwelt under his roof" (*RC* 25). He shrouded all his actions in silence, with an aura of deep contemplation.

Joseph is part of the communion of saints who are one with God and stand ready to be companions in faith now and in our final moments of life as they offer peace, consolation, and hope for eternal life. As part of this communion, Joseph, too, can help us achieve the interior peace that he experienced—a peace that can accompany us as we cross the threshold from time into eternity.

## Q When did Joseph die?

A It's impossible to know for certain when Joseph died, since the Gospels don't refer to it. By the time Jesus starts his public ministry, Joseph has disappeared. So all we know for sure is that Joseph lived at least until Jesus was twelve (Luke 2:42).

While Joseph scholars have a variety of ideas, most believe Joseph probably died around the time of Jesus' baptism and before the wedding feast in Cana, when Jesus was about thirty years old (Luke 3:23). That's because Mary is mentioned at the wedding feast in Cana but Joseph is not (John 2:1–12). And, while Jesus is preaching, those looking for him are only his "mother and brothers" (Matthew 12:46–49, Mark 3:32–34; Luke 8:19–21). Finally, while dying on the cross, Jesus entrusts his mother to the disciple, John, who took her to his home (John 19:27). If Joseph had been alive at the time, this wouldn't have been necessary.

## Q What was Saint Joseph's death like?

A While there is no reliable data regarding his death, we can assume that he must have died before Jesus, since Mary was given into the care of the disciple John at the crucifixion. So it's entirely likely that Joseph died with Jesus and Mary at his side, giving his death a place of great significance in popular devotion. From ancient times, Christians have viewed Joseph's death as placidly falling asleep in the arms of the Virgin and Jesus.

## Q Is that why Joseph is called the patron of a happy death?

A Yes. The origins of this thought can be seen as early as in the second century. At that time, the apocryphal book *The Story of Joseph the Carpenter* was used liturgically by the Judeo-Christians of Nazareth. In it, Jesus recounts to his disciples Joseph's entire life, and particularly his death. This story soon spread to Egypt, where the Coptic Monophysites instituted a feast to commemorate his death on August 2. From the influence of this book and this feast, Joseph eventually came to be considered "patron of a happy death," and icons depicting his death scene began to appear.

Confraternities were started to promote the devotion, and in 1909 Pius X approved the Litany of Saint Joseph, which included the invocations, "Hope of the Sick," "Patron of the Dying," and "Terror of Demons." In 1913, he inaugurated "The Pious Union of Saint Joseph's Passing for the Salvation of the Dying." In his 1920 *motu proprio* titled *Bonum Sane*, Pope Benedict XV also wanted Saint Joseph to be remembered as patron of the dying, since Joseph had passed away apparently attended by Jesus and Mary. The same pope approved two Votive Masses of Saint Joseph, one for the dying and another for a good death, as well as a prayer to obtain a happy death: "Like glorious Saint Joseph, may I die in the arms of Jesus and Mary...."

In the rite for anointing the sick found in *The Roman Ritual* of 1922, Pope Pius XI added the invocation, "May Saint Joseph, the dearest patron of the dying, strengthen your hope." He also composed the beautiful prayer, "I turn to you, Saint Joseph, patron of the dying...."

Q **Do we know anything about what happened to Saint Joseph after his death?**

A Saint Thomas Aquinas, Clement of Alexandria, Saint Bernardine of Sienna, and other theological writers believed that Joseph was one of the saints whose bodies rose from their graves at the time of Jesus' resurrection (Matthew 27:52–53). Given his importance as Jesus' father and Mary's husband, it's sensible that Joseph would deserve such an honor.

Other theologians, including Cornelius A Lapide and Francisco Suarez, believed that Joseph also went up to heaven body and soul at

Jesus' ascension (although Cardinal Prospero Lambertini, who later became Pope Benedict XIV, wrote that this could not be safely asserted).

In a 1960 homily, Pope John XXIII said that one could piously believe that Joseph and John the Baptist were among the first taken bodily to heaven with Christ, but this is not an article of faith that the Church has pronounced. Saint Bernardine of Sienna wrote, "We may believe out of devotion, but not with rash certainty, that Jesus decorated his presumed father with the same privilege granted to his most holy mother, so that as she was taken into heaven body and soul, so also on the day of Jesus' resurrection Saint Joseph was also raised with him."

## Life Links

### Examine

Are you prepared for the end of your life? Death doesn't always come with a great deal of advance notice. Sometimes it occurs swiftly and unexpectedly. How ready are you to leave this life and cross the threshold into eternity? What help can Saint Joseph offer?

### Connect

If you're like most people, you spend virtually no time thinking about death. It simply isn't a subject people want to consider. But this life will end before you know it, and you'll be required to present God everything that represents who you are. What will you present? Death is your connection to eternity. Spend this life connecting with God and the people he has brought into your life.

### Transform

Challenge yourself to maintain an eternal perspective—to view everything that occurs through the eyes of faith and eternity. This can dramatically change your world view and remind you that this life is temporary, God is in control, and heaven is your ultimate destination.

# CHAPTER EIGHT

# Joseph in Art

Q  Why is Joseph depicted so frequently in art, along with Jesus and Mary?

A  Since Joseph is one of the central figures of the salvation story, he is one of the biblical figures most often depicted in art, in addition to Jesus and Mary. He is almost always present in scenes of Jesus' birth in Bethlehem and is also pictured at Mary's side, dreaming in his sleep, holding Jesus in his arms, presenting the Child in the Temple, fleeing into Egypt, at his carpentry bench mentoring Jesus, in adoration before Jesus, or with a book in his hand teaching Jesus.

The ways in which Joseph is portrayed are as varied as the artists who render them. He is sometimes depicted as an old man with white hair and beard, staff or flowering rod in hand, halo over his head, perhaps with a lily in his right hand. Then again, we also see images of Joseph as a young man, jovial, happy, strong, peaceful, kind, and humble. Franco Zeffirelli captured this beautifully in his movie *Jesus of Nazareth* when he showed Joseph practicing his carpentry trade as an appealing and deeply religious family man.

## Q Why does art frequently portray Joseph as an old man?

A For many centuries, Joseph was seen as Mary's servant or guardian more than as her husband. This distortion came from the influence of the apocryphal stories, which attempted to defend Mary's virginity by making her husband into a frail, white-haired man in his nineties. This sends the false message that Mary and Joseph's virginity depended on the impotence of old age, rather than on virtue and the grace of God.

Today we know that Joseph probably married Mary when he was between eighteen and twenty-four, the age range that was customary for Hebrew youth, as explained in rabbinic texts. We can also surmise that God wanted his Son to enter human history in the most natural manner possible, within a family and with parents who would raise and educate him well. If Joseph were as old as he's often depicted, he would hardly have been able to fulfill his fatherly duties, let alone flee with Mary and Jesus into Egypt and cross the desert in a long, exhausting, and dangerous walk with little water. How could Joseph have supported Jesus and Mary without youthful strength?

## Q Do artists still depict Joseph as an elderly man?

A Thanks to ongoing study about the life of Joseph, modern artists have more information with which to inform their art and are less frequently depicting Joseph as an old man. The evangelist Luke described Jesus as "the son (as was supposed) of Joseph" (3:23). Most likely people would not have "supposed" him to be the son of a frail old man. Fortunately, artists in recent times seem to understand this idea more fully.

Q Why is Joseph sometimes shown with a flowering staff in his hand?

A In Numbers 17:17–26, it was the sprouting of Aaron's staff that indicated Aaron was chosen to serve at the Lord's dwelling. The staff is a sign of authority, the instrument for applying God's justice. By his staff sprouting, Aaron was divinely appointed to serve in the sanctuary.

Joseph was given a mission even more important than that of Aaron, serving "the sanctuary and the true tent [tabernacle] which is set up not by man but by the Lord" (Hebrews 8:2; 9:11, 24). If divine election was required to choose the servant of the old tabernacle, how much more was it necessary for God to choose the one who would serve the true tabernacle, the Lord Jesus.

Q Why do artists show Joseph's staff with almond blossoms and sometimes a lily?

A These symbols present two different aspects of Joseph's role as chosen by God and as husband of Mary.

The almond blossoms are a reflection of Aaron's staff, which flowered with almond blossoms (Numbers 17:19–23). Why almond? Because the Hebrew word for "almond" is very similar to the word for "watchfulness" or "vigilance." That is why God used the almond tree as a sign for Jeremiah to demonstrate his vigilance over his people (Jeremiah 1:10–11). In the New Testament, Joseph is the one who is called to watch over Jesus and Mary and to represent God's vigilance over them. More recently, scholars have looked at an additional interpretation that observes the almond within its protective shell as symbolizing Joseph's virtuous interior life hidden beneath his quiet surface.

The lily has long been a symbol of purity and chastity. In art, it signifies Joseph's God-given vocation to be Mary's husband and Jesus' father within the context of purity and virginity.

## Q Do some artistic images of Joseph stand out more than others?

A Yes. Some iconography of Saint Joseph is exceptional, not simply for its artistic beauty, but rather for the motif portrayed. For example, it is rare to find Joseph teaching Jesus the Torah or Law, even though this is in perfect harmony with the role that both the Bible and Hebrew tradition assigned to a father, that is, to teach his son the divine decrees. It is common to find depictions of Joseph in the carpenter shop with his tools, but it is rare to see him as one instructed in and knowledgeable of the Scriptures. This new vision began in Renaissance art (1450–1600), where he is shown not only holding a lily-staff, but also reading.

## Q So did Renaissance artists abandon traditional images of Joseph?

A No. In fact, there are some works that combine these images and show Joseph seated near his carpentry tools while reading a book. At least two well-known works (including a 1524 fresco and a painting by Giovanni Battista Moroni, d. 1578) show Joseph with a flowering staff in his right hand and a closed book in his left. It would seem that when these artists sought to express other details of Joseph's life, they didn't neglect his traditional features.

## Q Did Joseph-related artwork evolve alongside the study of Joseph?

A When the more in-depth studies of Joseph began taking shape, Joseph's image was often found in group scenes portraying Jesus' infancy. Then, as Christian thought began to focus on Joseph more directly, art gradually began to portray him in a more intimate relationship with the Holy Family, recognizing his mission as husband of Mary, father of Jesus, and head of the family.

A good example of this is a painting by Brother Gabriel Wüger, OSB (d. 1892), showing a young Joseph holding the Child and gazing serenely at him, as Jesus touches Joseph on the chest with one hand and on the face with the other in a gesture of love, trust, and admiration. While Joseph's fatherhood is clearly emphasized, his head is decorated with a halo, which signifies God's reward for his virtues. This painting also portrays Joseph with a flowering staff in his right hand, carpentry tools at his feet, and a lily symbolizing his purity and virginity.

## Q Has more recent art kept pace with the developments by Joseph scholars?

A Yes. For example, consider the large central fresco in the chapel of the General House of the Oblates of Saint Joseph in Rome. It was painted by Pagliardini of Rome in 1960, during preparation for the Second Vatican Council. The mural includes the verse, "Joseph gleams like a rainbow"—a reference to Sirach 50:7–8 and the symbol of God's covenant with his people after the Flood.

Since he is present when God makes his new covenant with mankind through his Son, Joseph is pictured at the center of the scene, holding the infant Jesus in his right arm and a lily in his left, symbolizing his chastity. The Child trustingly holds on to Joseph, whose expression reflects peaceful reassurance.

Two angels hold a ribbon with the phrase, "Let the heavenly court honor you, Joseph." To their left is the phrase, "Protector of Holy Church," and a depiction of John XXIII presenting Saint Peter's Basilica, representing the Church, to Joseph. (On March 19, 1961, this pope also named Joseph the protector of the Second Vatican Council.) The fresco also features images indicating Joseph's patronage over the Congregation of the Oblates of Saint Joseph. This artistic work is just one example of modern art being in harmony with current reflection on Joseph.

**Q** **Is Joseph honored at Saint Peter's Basilica at the Vatican in any special way?**

**A** Yes. On March 19, 1963, Pope John XXIII dedicated a new altar with an image of Joseph, protector of the Holy Church and also of the Second Vatican Council, giving him a central presence in the Vatican basilica. At this altar a Mass for peace is celebrated daily.

The basilica is also home to the 1647 mosaic "Saint Joseph's Dream," depicting the angel revealing to Joseph his role with regard to Mary's miraculous conception. And in 1851, a painting was placed in the Chapel of the Crucifix, picturing Joseph with the Child Jesus in his arms.

A beautiful statue of Joseph is located near the entrance to Saint Peter's Square, on the left side of Gian Lorenzo Bernini's Colonnade. It shows a robust man, with his eyes lifted to the sky, his right hand on his chest, and his left hand holding a flowering staff. Another image is in the vestibule of the basilica and portrays Joseph's death.

**Q** **Does secular art portray Joseph in the same way as biblical art?**

**A** No. However, cinema has portrayed Joseph quite effectively in several films, such as Franco Zeffirelli's 1977 *Jesus of Nazareth*, where Joseph's importance in the story of Jesus' Incarnation is highlighted, as well as his connection to Jesus' Davidic descent. These are essential to understanding Jesus as the Christ or Messiah. While the film is not completely factual, Zeffirelli does a good job of presenting Joseph as young and handsome, fulfilling his mission as Jesus' father and Mary's protector within a normal family, working as a carpenter.

Another movie, Catherine Hardwicke's 2006 *The Nativity Story*, portrays Joseph's role in an inspiring manner. He is a hard worker, kind and generous, heroically compassionate, courageous, and self-sacrificing. He protects and provides for Mary and Jesus in every difficult situation. While this film, too, has its weaknesses, it helps viewers appreciate the historical customs of betrothal and marriage. It shows

Mary and Joseph's special calling and the tenderness that springs from the faith they share. Their lives are united to receive the Son of God.

Q  **Has Joseph been remembered in music?**

A  Yes, in quite a few ways. Some well-known composers created Masses in his honor, such as Johann G. Albrechtsberger ("Saint Joseph Mass"), Flor Peeters ("Mass in Honor of Saint Joseph"), and Pergolesi ("Panegyric on the Death of Saint Joseph"). Countless other musical compositions and popular songs demonstrate love and veneration for Joseph in countries around the world.

Q  **Has Joseph been honored in other ways beyond art, film, and music?**

A  Yes. Devotion to Saint Joseph has been officially expressed by the canonical crowning of his image. This took place in Bogotá, Colombia, in 1779; México City in 1788; Guanajuato, México, in 1790; Kalisz, Poland, in 1796 and 1895; and many other places around the world.

Apparitions of Saint Joseph have also been reported, most notably in Novara, Italy, in 1448; Knock, Ireland, in 1879; and Fatima, Portugal, in 1917.

# Life Links

## Examine

What kind of images have you seen of Joseph over the years? How have these images informed your understanding of Joseph? What can you do to incorporate other understandings of Joseph into the ones you currently hold?

## Connect

Go to an art museum and meditate on images of the Holy Family and of Joseph. Notice the symbols and their meaning. Sit or stand before one of the images of Joseph. Reflect on the image. What is the story? What are the relationships you see? How can the image support your faith more fully?

## Transform

If you want to advance in holiness, surround yourself with holy images. As we learn the different images of Joseph that inform our ideas of him, we can transform our understanding into action.

# CHAPTER NINE

# Saint Joseph, Model and Intercessor

**Q** How can Joseph help families?

**A** As "protector of the Church," Joseph is also considered the protector of families. So Joseph's protection extends to our families today. The family is a reflection of God's love for his people and Christ's love for his Church. Just as Joseph demonstrated his love for the Holy Family, he will help us do the same for ours. In reality, the family of Nazareth, of which he is the head, has become one of best models for all families. All families can consider him their protector.

**Q** Is Joseph considered an especially powerful intercessor?

**A** Numerous saints and spiritual authors testify to the effectiveness of Joseph's intercession, including the great theologian Saint Thomas Aquinas, who teaches that "certain saints were given the privilege of protecting us in particular circumstances, but Saint Joseph was charged with interceding for us in all our needs." The great devotee of Saint Joseph, Saint Teresa of Ávila, says that: "whatever Saint Joseph asks is done in heaven." The founder of the Oblates of Saint Joseph, Saint Joseph Marello, so trusted in Saint Joseph's intercessory power that he declared, "If Saint Joseph did not grant us favors, he would no longer be Saint Joseph." It is in the light of this intercessory power that Pope Benedict XV considered that the devotees of Saint Joseph have the easiest path to holiness, and that Pius IX, himself a great devotee of Jesus' father, pronounced that his intercession before God was "all-powerful."

Q Can Joseph also be thought of as a protector?

A Yes. In fact, in 1870, Pope Pius IX proclaimed Joseph as "patron of the universal Church," since God had chosen Joseph as Jesus' father. In 1889, Pope Leo XIII explained the reason for Joseph's patronage over the Catholic Church in these words: "The special motives for which Saint Joseph has been proclaimed patron of the Church, and from which the Church looks for singular benefit from his patronage and protection, are that Joseph was the spouse of Mary and that he was reputed as the father of Jesus Christ. From these sources have sprung his dignity, his holiness, his glory."

Joseph is also considered the protector of priests, since he was called to care for God's divine treasure here on earth, living intimately with him, holding him, supporting him, defending and educating him. As Pius IX taught, Joseph "most diligently reared him whom the faithful were to receive as the bread that came down from heaven." So there has always been a powerful connection between the mission of Joseph and the mission of the ordained priest.

## *Q* Do other groups also consider Joseph their protector?

*A* Yes. Many religious congregations, secular institutes, and societies of apostolic life have Joseph as their patron, a relationship supported by the faithful throughout the world. This includes numerous confraternities, lay societies, and institutions named after Joseph. All of these demonstrate the great love and respect Christians have long held for Joseph.

## *Q* Who are the Oblates of Saint Joseph?

*A* The Oblates of Saint Joseph are a congregation founded by Saint Joseph Marello, who was inspired by Joseph's life of complete dedication to serving the interests of Jesus. In 1872, at the age of twenty-seven, Marello envisioned a "company of Saint Joseph to promote the interests of Jesus." Each member of the company would draw "inspiration from his exemplar Saint Joseph, who was the first on earth to look after the interests of Jesus." The company would be open to anyone who desired "to follow the Divine Master more closely by the observance of the Evangelical Counsels," by withdrawing into the house of Saint Joseph with "the resolve to remain hidden and silently active in imitation of that great model of a poor and obscure life."

Marello's idea became a reality in 1878, when he founded the congregation and named its members "Oblates of Saint Joseph." (The word "Oblate" indicates a person offered or dedicated.) Today, its special purpose remains to honor and love Joseph by imitating his virtues and spreading his devotion. The Oblates' 500 members are spread throughout the world, each dedicated to reproducing Joseph's virtues in his own life, in union with God, in humility, in hiddenness, in hard work, in service to the Church, in dedication to the interests of Jesus. As Marello frequently said to his religious, "Let us ask Saint Joseph to be our spiritual director."

**Q Do I need to become an Oblate of Saint Joseph in order to imitate his example?**

*A* No. All Christians can look to Joseph as the perfect example of being totally and humbly available to God's will. As John Paul II wrote in *Redemptoris Custos*, every Christian should draw "'what is new and what is old' (Matthew 13:52) from the storehouse of the noble figure of Joseph" (*RC* 17). Joseph is the model of unconditional obedience to God's call. His was the purest "obedience of faith" (Romans 1:5; 16:26) as the first depositary of the divine mystery. He is also "the first to be placed by God on the path of Mary's 'pilgrimage of faith'...a path along which...Mary will precede in a perfect way" (*RC* 5).

Joseph is an example for those looking for a deeper, richer interior life, because he "was in daily contact with the mystery 'hidden from ages past,' and which dwelt under his roof" (*RC* 25). Yet all of his actions were performed in silence, within the context of deep contemplation.

Many saints drew inspiration from Joseph. While it's impossible to list them all, the list would certainly include: Saint Francis de Sales, Saint Aloysius Gonzaga, Saint John Marie Vianney, Saint John Baptist de la Salle, Saint Teresa, Saint Alphonsus Liguori, Saint Vincent de Paul, and Saint Joseph Marello. Needless to say, Joseph has been a major influence for many saints. Imitating his example is like attending a school of holiness.

# Life Links

### Examine

Have you ever sought the help of Joseph's intercessory power of prayer? While you can't always change your circumstances, Joseph can intervene for you and ask God to provide you the grace to persevere through the toughest of situations. Then, patiently let God ease your burdens in his way and his timing, rather than dictating how you think it should be done.

### Connect

Joseph's focus has always been on the will, the response, and the solution God offers. He'll seek the graces you need and help you live a holier life. Connecting to Joseph means having complete trust in his ability to obtain answers to your prayers and to protect you along the course of your spiritual journey to the Father.

### Transform

What an amazing opportunity you have to bring Joseph into your life. You have the power of his intercession and the promise of his protection from the enemy, both of which help you become renewed in every aspect of your life: in the home, in your church, and in the world.

# CHAPTER TEN

# Honoring and Studying Saint Joseph

**Q** **How did devotion to Joseph develop through the centuries?**

**A** Devotion to Joseph can be traced back to at least the year 670, when Arculf, bishop of Gaul, reported that there was a church in Nazareth built over the house in which Jesus was raised, and another at the spot where the angel Gabriel made his annunciation to Mary. There is also a reference to Joseph in Bethlehem at the Basilica of the Nativity, which bears the inscription IVM (*Ioseph Virum Mariae*, "Joseph, husband of Mary"). There is also a small church dedicated to Joseph built atop the ruins of a more ancient church in Bethlehem.

In Europe, devotion to Joseph is recorded as far back as the ninth and tenth centuries, beginning in Germany and Italy and spreading to numerous centers, basilicas, churches, chapels, abbeys, convents, and monasteries dedicated to Joseph. In the centuries since, so many churches have been dedicated to Joseph in so many parts of the world that it's impossible to list them here.

**Q** Why didn't the Church give him more attention during the early centuries?

**A** During the first centuries, the Church's attention was focused on defining the identity of Jesus Christ. This required reflection on Mary, his Mother, in order to proclaim Jesus' divinity. Joseph was mainly mentioned only when analyzing the infancy of Jesus in the Gospel texts.

**Q** What has the leadership of the Church, the magisterium, said about Joseph?

**A** The leaders of the Church are big Joseph fans, too! Pope Pius IX extended the feast of the Patronage of Saint Joseph to the whole Church, by issuing a decree on September 10, 1847, *Inclytus Patriarcha Joseph*. On December 8, 1870, he also proclaimed Joseph to be patron of the universal (Catholic) Church, with the decree *Quemadmodum Deus*. Pope Leo XIII placed his pontificate under the "most powerful protection of Saint Joseph," and referred to Saint Joseph in numerous documents, and especially in his encyclical *Quamquam Pluries*. Likewise, Popes Pius X and Benedict XV proclaimed Joseph's importance in their documents.

On March 19, 1928, Pope Pius XI gave Joseph precedence over Saint John the Baptist and Saint Peter, and referred to his intercession as "all-powerful."

Pope Pius XII praised aspects of Joseph in several documents. In 1956, he described Jesus' relationship with Joseph, emphasizing that Jesus' heart beat with love for the father he obeyed and assisted in the carpentry shop.

Joseph was named protector of the Second Vatican Ecumenical Council in 1961 by Pope John XXIII.

Pope Paul VI often presented a clear and inspiring image of Joseph, pointing out that in the eucharistic sacrifice we venerate Mary and Joseph first of all. Paul VI also highlighted Joseph's relationship with the world of work, presented him as part of God's plan for the redemption of mankind, and as the reference point for families.

Blessed John Paul II placed Joseph at the heart of our redemption and proclaimed him as a model for all pastors and ministers in the Church in his first encyclical of 1979. In 1981, he put Joseph alongside Jesus in "the Gospel of work." Most significantly, in 1989, Pope John Paul II issued the apostolic exhortation *Redemptoris Custos*—a real treatise illustrating the person and mission of Joseph in the life of Christ and the Church. This document is the magisterium's most complete pronouncement on Joseph to date.

Pope Benedict XVI has also made repeated references to Joseph. For example, in 2006 he reflected on how Joseph carried out his mission in great humility.

### Q When did simple devotion to Joseph evolve into a full field of systematic study?

*A* Josephology first appeared at the beginning of the thirteenth century, when Saint Bonaventure highlighted Joseph's role in his *Commentary on Saint Luke*, and later in some of his sermons. Saint Bernardine of Sienna did the same thing in his *Sermon on Saint Joseph, Husband of the Blessed Virgin Mary*, where he suggests that Joseph was resurrected and ascended into heaven.

As Josephology took root, Jean Charlier (better known as Gerson, d. 1419) emerged as one of its great teachers. Chancellor of the University of Paris, his influential works included *Considerations on Saint Joseph, Josefina*, and the *Sermon on the Glorious Birth of the Virgin Mary and on Honoring Her Virginal Husband Joseph*.

Another great Josephologist was Isidore Isolani (d. 1528), who produced the theological treatise on Joseph: *Summa de Donis Sancti Ioseph*. Francis Suarez (d. 1617) revolutionized reflection on Joseph by elevating him to a member of the hypostatic union (the union of divine and human natures in Jesus). Additionally, hundreds more theologians have written in defense of Joseph's privileges, making Josephology a rich and rewarding field of study.

**Q** How has Josephology evolved from the thirteenth century into the twenty-first?

**A** The modern international interest in Josephology can be traced back to the First Congress of Saint Joseph Studies, organized in 1945 at the Shrine of San José de la Montaña in Barcelona, Spain. Two years later, in 1947, the Discalced Carmelite Fathers of Valladolid, Spain, began publication of *Estudios Josefinos*, the first scholarly journal dedicated to studying Joseph. Then in 1951, these same Carmelites created the Iberian-American Josephology Society, which included the Spanish- and Portuguese-speaking nations of Central and South America. Led by Father José Antonio Carrasco, OCD, this society was so successful that similar ones began popping up in other countries.

The Saint Joseph Information and Research Center was founded in 1952 at the Oratory of Saint Joseph in Montreal, and by 1953 it began publication of the journal *Cahiers de Joséphologie*. As this developed, in 1962 Father Roland Gauthier, CSC, founded the North American Josephology Society in Canada.

In 1981, when the Josephite movement arose in Rome, another important milestone in the study and veneration of Joseph was established by the Oblates of Saint Joseph. Following publication of the groundbreaking *Redemptoris Custos*, the Guardian of the Redeemer Meeting Point was opened—a center for Josephite formation for priests, religious, and laity.

Centers devoted to the study of Joseph were soon being established around the world. Among the most notable centers are: the Kalisz Josephology Study Center in Poland, the Saint Joseph Information and Study Center of México, the Central American Center of Research and Promotion of Saint Joseph in El Salvador, and the Josephite Spirituality Center in Brazil. Today, all of these centers regularly publish studies on Joseph.

$Q$  **Who are some of the people most responsible for promoting devotion to Saint Joseph?**

$A$  Countless people have championed a devotion to Joseph throughout the centuries. A list of the most noteworthy people would include Saint Teresa of Ávila (d. 1582), who spread devotion to Joseph throughout all of Spain and dedicated eleven Carmelite monasteries to his patronage. Saint Francis de Sales (d. 1622) contributed greatly to the spread of devotion to Joseph through his sermons and writings, particularly *The Spiritual Conferences*. The Servite Alexis-Henri-Marie Cardinal Lépicier (d. 1936) wrote the *Tractatus de Sancto Joseph* and was appointed by Pope Pius X to help prepare approval of the Litany of Saint Joseph. Finally, Saint Joseph Marello (d. 1895), founder of the Oblates of Saint Joseph, inspired devotion to Joseph.

$Q$  **Is Joseph honored by organizations other than churches?**

$A$  Yes. Joseph is also venerated by countless confraternities and arch-confraternities, monastic communities, religious congregations, and lay societies. One ancient example is the Arch-Confraternity of Saint Joseph, established in 1345 at Rabat on the Isle of Malta.

$Q$  **Is Joseph remembered in other ways?**

$A$  Yes. There are a many countries, regions, cities, and dioceses that have chosen Joseph as their protector. In 1665, Ferdinand III declared him patron of the kingdom of Bohemia. In 1675, he was chosen as patron of the Austrian dominions, and in 1676 patron of the Germanic territories. He later became protector of China, Spain, Peru, and the Philippines.

Countless towns and cities have named Joseph as their patron, including Naples, Genoa, Turin, Florence, Verona, Venice, Palermo, Avignon, Manila, and Krakow. In Brazil alone there are over ninety municipalities bearing his name, and since Joseph was patron of the

California missionary expedition, the state's first secular city still bears the name San José.

Numerous dioceses also have him as their protector, some of which are Orvieto, Ottawa, Włocławek, Liverpool, San José in California, San José in Costa Rica, Caacupé in Paraguay, Cúcuta in Colombia, Maracay in Venezuela, Santa Fe in Argentina, Tapachula in México, and in Brazil the dioceses of Fortaleza, Mariana, Garanhuns, Macapá, Campo Mourão, and São José dos Campos. We could go on all day, but we hope this sampling gives you an idea of how Joseph's name has spread far and wide throughout the world.

### Q How has Joseph been recognized and celebrated in the liturgy?

A The earliest liturgical feast appears to belong to Egyptian Coptics of the Eastern Church, which celebrates "The Death of Saint Joseph," or "The Stay of the Holy Family in Egypt" on August 2 (Abîb 26 in their calendar). Other Eastern observances in the Byzantine Church include "The Holy Forefathers from Abraham to Joseph" on the Sunday before Christmas, "Mary and her Husband Joseph" on December 26, and "Joseph, David, and James" on the Sunday after Christmas. Syrian churches also celebrate "The Revelation to Joseph" on the second Sunday before Christmas.

In the West, March 19 has been observed as the feast of Saint Joseph. The *Code of Canon Law* includes this "Solemn Commemoration of Saint Joseph, Husband of the Blessed Virgin Mary" among the Church's holy days of obligation.

Another liturgical feast is the Patronage of Saint Joseph, a solemn celebration that has been observed by the Carmelites since 1680, and later followed by the Augustinians, Mercedarians, and Barnabites. In 1703, the Diocese of México began observing this feast—a practice that spread to many other dioceses such as Puebla, Los Angeles, Palermo, De La Plata, Pavia, Cologne, Orvieto, Asti, and Acqui. In 1847, Pope Pius IX extended this feast to the entire Church for the third Sunday after Easter.

In 1956, after the institution of the new feast of Saint Joseph the Worker for May 1, the feast of the Patronage of Saint Joseph was abolished. However, the title "Patron of the Universal Church" was preserved by adding it to the feast of March 19, up until the liturgical revisions of 1969.

Joseph is also honored on the solemnity of March 19, "Saint Joseph, Husband of the Blessed Virgin Mary"; the feast of May 1, "Saint Joseph the Worker"; and the Votive Mass of Saint Joseph, as well as included in the "feast of the Holy Family of Jesus, Mary, and Joseph," which is usually celebrated on the Sunday after Christmas.

Certain dioceses and religious congregations celebrate additional feasts of their own, such as the "Finding in the Temple," the "Flight into Egypt," and, most importantly, the "Espousals" or the "Feast of the Holy Spouses."

In addition to the Mass texts for his feasts, Joseph is mentioned in the "Litany of the Saints," and since 1884 his name has been included in the prayers for after Mass. Pope Leo XIII prescribed a beautiful prayer to Joseph to be recited after the rosary, "To you, Saint Joseph, we come in our trials." In 1919, Pope Benedict XV approved a proper preface for Saint Joseph feasts, and in 1921, a more solemn chant was provided for it. In 1922, Pope Pius XI included Joseph in the prayers for the dying that are found in the Roman ritual. And in 1962, John XXIII inserted Joseph's name into the Eucharistic Prayer of the Mass.

## Q Are there any prayers or devotional practices related to Joseph that carry indulgences?

*A* There are several, but the most noteworthy include the "Litany of Saint Joseph," to which Pope Pius X attached an indulgence in 1909, and "The Little Office of Saint Joseph," to which Pope Benedict XV granted a special indulgence in 1921. Many other prayers are accompanied by indulgences, such as the well-known "Jesus, Mary, and Joseph, I give you my heart and my soul...." What's important about all of these prayers is that they honor Joseph's holiness, dignity, and specific mission in the mystery of our redemption.

*Q* **Are there special prayers and practices related to Joseph that have developed?**

*A* Yes. There are quite a few. Some of these include:

+ "The Seven Sorrows and Joys of Saint Joseph" have been in use since the eighteenth century, with roots going back to the sixteenth century based on concepts introduced by Saint John Chysostom (d. 407). (See "Prayers to Saint Joseph," page 113.)

+ A "Daily Litany of Saint Joseph" had been published in Rome by 1597, and is still very common. It is attributed to Jerónimo Gracián of the Mother of God. (See the author's own translation in "Prayers to Saint Joseph," page 112.)

+ A "Saint Joseph Rosary" was in use by the end of the fifteenth century. In the years since, many forms of it have arisen, including the one that has been used since 1991 by the California province of the Oblates of Saint Joseph. (See "Prayers to Saint Joseph," page 109.)

+ The Belgian Augustinians began using the "Saint Joseph Cincture" in 1659, while praying for physical healing and protection from Satan, and Pope Pius IX later attached indulgences to its use.

+ The Solemn Novena of Saint Joseph was being celebrated in preparation for the March 19 feast by 1713, at the Jesuit Church of Saint Ignatius in Rome.

+ The entire month of March was consecrated in honor of Joseph in Modena by 1802.

✦ The "Scapular of the Blessed Virgin Mary, Saint Joseph and Saint Camillus" was introduced by the Camillian Fathers in 1865, followed in 1880 by the Holy See's approval of a "Saint Joseph Scapular."

✦ In México in 1875, the custom of blessing candles on Saint Joseph Day came into practice, followed in 1903 by the blessing of "Saint Joseph Water."

✦ By 1876, the Marist Teaching Brothers were commemorating Joseph every Wednesday, which is still considered his special day of the week. Other similar observances still exist today, such as the "Perpetual Novena to Saint Joseph," the "Seven Sundays of Saint Joseph," the "Nineteen Wednesdays of Saint Joseph," and the "Nineteenth Day of the Month."

*Q* **Has Joseph become a part of cultural traditions?**

*A* People have expressed their affection for Joseph In many places around the world. For example:

✦ On March 19 in Sicily, people organize the "Saint Joseph Table" and invite the poor to dine with them. An elderly man is dressed as Joseph, who blesses the guests with his flowering staff. This custom has spread in some forms to other countries, including the United States.

✦ In other places, people bring loaves of bread to churches to be blessed and distributed to the poor.

✦ On May 1, in Gela, Italy, it is customary to bring to church a "Saint Joseph Dish" filled with various types of food that are then auctioned off and the proceeds given to charity.

+ In Riccia, Italy, people express their devotion to Joseph by inviting three people to lunch: a married couple and a young boy, representing the Holy Family.

+ In Siracusa, Italy, twelve devotees of Joseph each prepare three large ring-shaped loaves along with several small ones on the nineteenth of each month, and then offer them before an image of Joseph during the Mass. The three large loaves are given to an elderly man, a young woman, and a child, while the smaller ones are given to friends.

+ In several places, families prepare a plentiful table on March 19 and invite five guests representing Jesus, Mary, Joseph, Joachim, and Anne, or they prepare it for the poor in a public park.

+ On January 23, the Feast of the Betrothal of Mary and Joseph, there is a custom of having sweets and baked goods blessed, then shared with friends or the sick.

+ People bring "Saint Joseph Violets" on Saint Joseph's feast in Naples and present them before Joseph's image in church or in their homes.

+ Another custom is to have processions start from two churches, one carrying a statue of Joseph and the other a statue of Mary. When the two processions meet at the main square, Mary offers a bouquet of flowers to Joseph.

+ In Brazil, many churches celebrate the Novena of Saint Joseph on the nineteenth of each month by having their members bring food, tea, and flowers to be blessed.

*Q* **What are some other popular beliefs about Joseph?**

*A* The local customs often stem from some interesting beliefs about Joseph. Examples include:

+ In Scotland, Joseph is considered patron of the weather. His statue is placed outside the home and covered with an umbrella or other device to indicate the desired weather.

+ In northeastern Brazil, he is thought to be the saint who sends rain. If it does not rain on Saint Joseph's Day (March 19), many believe it will be a drought year. But if it does rain on or near that day, they believe the weather will be favorable and bring a good harvest. On this day, people march in procession and set off fireworks.

+ Joseph competes with Saint Anthony for the title of holy matchmaker.

+ Since the eighteenth century in Brazil, pregnant women have appealed to Joseph as they also invoke our Lady of a Good Delivery.

+ In northeastern Brazil, Joseph is invoked as protector of a good marriage and for the avoidance of an unhappy marriage.

+ Throughout the United States, people often locate a small statue or medal of Saint Joseph on a property they wish to sell or be able to purchase.

+ In California, Saint Joseph is venerated as patron of the Unborn. People come to his shrine in Santa Cruz for post-abortion healing, and for consolation following a miscarriage.

*Q* **How is new thought and information about Joseph being discovered?**

*A* Josephology study centers have been established around the world. These centers actively publish Josephological studies containing the latest research, thought, and information. National Josephite study weeks are also held, where scholarly studies are presented. Many of these studies are listed in Father Roland Gauthier's huge bibliography on Saint Joseph and the Holy Family, which lists over 19,000 publications.

In 1970, Josephology scholars from all over the world gathered in Rome for the First International Saint Joseph Symposium to present their research into *Saint Joseph in the First Fifteen Centuries of the Church*. Since then, these international symposia have been held approximately every four years:

+ The Second International Saint Joseph Symposium in Toledo, Spain, in 1976, on *Saint Joseph in the Renaissance (1450–1600)*

+ The Third in Montreal, Canada, in 1980, on *Saint Joseph in the Seventeenth Century*

+ The Fourth in Kalisz, Poland, in 1985, again on *Saint Joseph in the Seventeenth Century*

+ The Fifth in México City in 1989, covering the eighteenth century

+ The Sixth in Rome in 1993, on the nineteenth century

+ The Seventh in Malta in 1997, on the nineteenth and twentieth centuries

+ The Eighth in El Salvador in 2001, on *Theological and Pastoral Aspects of Redemptoris Custos*

✦ The Ninth in Kevalaer, Germany, in 2005, on *Saint Joseph's Role in Salvation History*

✦ The Tenth in Kalisz in 2009, on *Saint Joseph, Patron for Our Times.*

The volumes of research coming out of these symposia form an excellent collection of reliable information about Joseph that places him solidly in relationship with Christ and within the heart of the Church.

### $Q$ What is the history of Joseph in relation to the Church in North America?

$A$ Joseph's veneration in North America began with Franciscan missionaries such as Fray Pedro de Gante, who brought devotion to Joseph as a major ingredient of Catholic evangelization in "New Spain" (including what is now México). By the late 1520s, the first parish for Native Americans was built in México City and named "San José de Belén de los Naturales"—often described as "the cradle of Christianity in the Americas." The first school for American Indians was also placed under Joseph's protection. In 1555, Joseph was declared patron of the ecclesiastical province of the Archdiocese of México and its nine suffragan dioceses, which led to Joseph's patronage over all of New Spain.

Throughout New Spain, both Franciscan and Jesuit evangelizers founded Saint Joseph missions, such as San José Comundú in Baja, California, in 1708; San José de los Nasonis in Eastern Texas in 1716; San José Aguayo, "the queen of the Texas missions," in 1720; San José del Cabo in Baja, California, in 1730; and San José in Alta California, in 1797. Several of the earliest Spanish secular cities were also named for Joseph: San José de la Laguna in New México in 1699; San José in Arizona (now known as Tucson) in 1762; and San José, the first secular city in California, in 1777.

Similarly for "New France" (including what is now French Canada), Joseph was made its patron in 1624. In 1639, Blessed Marie of the Incarnation (the first female missionary to the New World) established an Ursuline cloister named for Jesus, Mary, and Joseph. In 1641, the first church in Canada to be dedicated to Joseph was founded for the Hurons at Fort Saint Mary in Midland, Ontario. Father Pierre Chaumonot introduced the cincture of the Holy Family and founded Holy Family confraternities at Montreal and Quebec. In 1649, the Jesuits founded Mission Saint Joseph on the Isle of Saint Joseph in upper Lake Huron as a place of refuge for the Hurons. In 1665, Blessed François Montmorency de Laval, the first apostolic vicar of French Canada, allowed the Association of the Holy Family to celebrate the feast of the Espousals, and later as bishop, in 1684, he extended the feast to the whole diocese and moved it to the third Sunday after Easter.

Additionally, Lake Michigan was originally named Lake Saint Joseph, influenced by missions in southeast Michigan. Eventually, devotion to Joseph in French Canada led a religious brother, Saint André Bessette, to found the Oratory of Saint Joseph in Montreal in 1904. This oratory has since grown into the largest shrine to Joseph in the world.

In the North American British colonies, Saint Joseph's Church, built in Philadelphia in 1733, was the first Catholic church and was significant in establishing religious freedom. Later, Saint Joseph College was also established there, eventually becoming Saint Joseph's University.

In 1810, Saint Elizabeth Ann Seton founded the Saint Joseph Free School, as well as Saint Joseph Academy, both of which formed the cradle of Catholic education in the United States. In 1811, Frances Allen, the daughter of atheist Ethan Allen, was the first woman born in New England to become a nun, crediting both her conversion and her religious vocation to Joseph.

In 1816, the cornerstone was laid for Saint Joseph Proto-Cathedral in Bardstown, Kentucky, the first cathedral west of the Allegheny

Mountains. In 1844, Saint Joseph Church was blessed in St. Louis, Missouri, and eventually was declared a shrine following Joseph's protection during the cholera epidemic of 1866.

On the West Coast in 1768, Joseph was chosen as patron of the Spanish expedition to Alta California. When the military leaders were discouraged over the lack of supplies and were ready to abandon the mission, the great missionary Junipero Serra convinced them to pray a novena to Joseph. Miraculously, on March 19, 1770 (Saint Joseph Day), the supply ship was sighted. This date marks the establishment of the colony of New California.

A painting given to Mission Dolores in San Francisco around 1780 shows Joseph as patron of the missions, holding the Child, with King Carlos IV and Pope Pius VI kneeling reverently before them. Also, in 1803, the first Saint Joseph Church was built in San José, which is now home to Saint Joseph Cathedral.

## Q What is Joseph's recent history of devotion in the United States?

*A* In 1923, the shrine parish of Saint Joseph in Pontiac, Michigan, was founded for Polish immigrants. In 1924, the Shrine of Saint Joseph in Stirling, New Jersey, was established. In 1947, Saint Joseph's Grove was completed at the National Shrine of Our Sorrowful Mother in Portland, Oregon, where there are marble panels of the Seven Sorrows and Joys of Joseph. In 1933, the Oblates of Saint Joseph opened Saint Joseph's Seminary and Chapel in Santa Cruz, California, now also home to the Shrine of Saint Joseph, Guardian of the Redeemer.

In the 1950s, American Jesuit Father Francis Filas began publishing detailed scholarly studies on Joseph. Others followed in the footsteps of this pioneer, including Dominican Fathers Timothy Sparks, Jim Davis, and Basil Cole; as well as Father Joseph Chorpenning, Oblate of Saint Francis de Sales; Dr. Carolyn C. Wilson; and the Oblates of Saint Joseph.

In recent decades, many ministry groups have formed under Joseph's patronage, including: the Sisters of Saint Joseph the Worker in the Diocese of Covington, Kentucky, in 1973; the Apostolate for Family Consecration in Ohio in 1975; the Holy Spouses Society of the Oblates in California in 1992; the Men of Saint Joseph in New Hampshire in 1993; Saint Joseph Covenant Keepers in Florida in 1994; and Saint Joseph, Patron of the Unborn, in Santa Cruz, California, in 2001.

Today in the United States, there are about fifteen cathedrals named for Joseph, as well as numerous Saint Joseph churches. Additionally, there are many traditional and modern devotions to Joseph in different areas of the country.

If you'd like more information than what you've found in these questions and answers, you are encouraged to explore the resources available at the Oblate Center in Santa Cruz, California, that includes: *Guardian of the Redeemer*, a quarterly magazine; the osjoseph.org Web site; and Guardian of the Redeemer Bookstore.

# Life Links

## Examine

Would you like to learn more about Joseph? What would you most like to learn? Are you willing to read a bit more each day? Many people have studied the life of Joseph, and you can continue that tradition. As you do, Joseph can become more and more a part of your life. From daily Scripture and spiritual reading you can learn more each day about how to grow in holiness in the image of Jesus, Mary, and Joseph.

## Connect

When you absorb the Bible and good spiritual books, you establish a direct link to the classroom of personal growth as a child of God. Consider starting the daily practice of reading about Joseph and praying some of the devotions found in the back of this book. With each page you turn, you can learn just a little bit more.

## Transform

If you make an effort to learn as much about God and grow in your wisdom and knowledge of him, you can more fully understand the incredibly humbling experience of having a personal relationship with your heavenly Father. Let Joseph help you and be your guide.

# Q & A Conclusion

We hope these questions and answers have helped you learn more about one of the most unique men who ever lived, Joseph of Nazareth. We hope he has become more real and more accessible to you. Beyond that, we pray that you'll want to pursue an ongoing relationship with him—not just as protector, intercessor, or father figure—but also as a real partner for your life. Few things are more comforting along the bumpy road of life than to have Joseph as your supportive guide. Not only will he help you smooth out your journey, but he will help you stay on course and avoid the dangerous detours of temptation and sin.

In each of the Life Links sections, you probably noticed a common formula:

**Examine, Connect, and Transform.** The next step is to connect with him on a daily basis and transform your life into the person God wants you to be, do all that he wants you to accomplish, and live out the unique vocation and mission he has given you.

If that's your desire—to be connected and united with Joseph—you can also consider becoming consecrated to Jesus through him.

What is consecration to Joseph?

Consecration is an important act in the life of a Christian. The scriptural term means "becoming sanctified or holy." In the Gospels, Jesus is consecrated to the Father: "And for their sake I consecrate myself, that they also may be consecrated in truth" (John 17:19). So our consecration is rooted in Christ's own consecration. Dedicating our life to Jesus is the primary consecration and covenant for every follower of Christ, and it begins in baptism.

All other consecrations are secondary and are good only to the extent that they help us follow Christ and his teachings more faithfully. Just as Mary and Joseph were united by the bond of marriage, so there is a bond uniting consecration to Mary and consecration to Joseph.

In Scripture, both Mary and Joseph completely dedicated their lives to Jesus. So when we consecrate ourselves to either Mary or Joseph, we establish a permanent and ongoing relationship completely dedicated to the service and interests of Christ. The result? We have their prayers for divine help in fulfilling our personal vocation to holiness and our mission in life.

It's not enough just to pray a consecration prayer, however. It's essential to live it in our daily lives. Such a prayer should lead us to active collaboration, personal imitation, and following the example of Joseph and Mary in devoting our life to Christ. When that happens, who we are and what we do can more fully become a reflection of life within the Holy Family.

In our consecration to Mary, we ask the mother of the Redeemer to be our mother in time and eternity. In the same way, in our consecration to Joseph, we ask the guardian of the Redeemer to be our guardian, not just for a passing moment, but also for all time and eternity.

Joseph knows how to make our house a holy place. He wants Jesus to be the center of families. Joseph is also the master craftsman in God's workshop of human life—after all, it's the trade he knows best. Joseph knows a lot about how to help us grow in our faith through the abundant life of grace that flows from Jesus Christ. His workshop in Nazareth can become our workshop now when we choose to be his apprentices, accepting his guardianship and guidance in our life. This is done by consecrating our lives to Jesus through Joseph. He will never fail us or let us down:

**Joseph can pray for us.** He is a powerful intercessor on our behalf and will go to his son, Jesus, with our needs.

**Joseph can lead us** in prayer and show us how to pray, often using silence as his classroom, so that we can better hear God's call. We can learn how to go beyond asking for God's help in our needs—and move to adoration, thanksgiving, praise, listening, and contemplating Christ in sacred Scripture and devotions (for example, the Sacred Heart of Jesus, Immaculate Heart of Mary).

**Joseph can teach us** what we need to learn about life—such as purity of body, mind, and spirit—and the value of simplicity and responsibility. He is the model of authentic manhood and will show us what it means to be a man of God, an important reality for both men and women to understand.

**Joseph can guide us** in and through situations, events, and relationships. As a devoted father, he will be there when we need him and will watch over us with his kind heart united to the heart of Mary, his spouse.

**Joseph can equip us** with the skills we need to get through life, particularly in raising children. Joseph knows what we need and will see that our needs are met.

**Joseph can protect us** from the devil and sins of the flesh. Known as the terror of demons, he is a most capable adversary of Satan and is fully prepared to face him without hesitation or fear.

**Joseph can work with us,** side-by-side, not just in our job, but also in all that comprises our lifework in the home, in church, and in the world. Pope John Paul II reminds us that "work was the daily expression of love in the life of the Family of Nazareth" (*RC* 22), and so should it be for us. The use of our talents and skills can be expressions of love that bring glory to God—whether we use those talents and skills in the home, the workplace, the Church, the world, or in any other relationship or setting.

\*\*\*

If you're committed to allowing Joseph to guide you and draw you into a more intimate relationship with Jesus Christ, you can pray the following Act of Consecration each day. In this way, you can entrust yourself to one of the best-known saints, our beloved Joseph.

\*\*\*

After the Act of Consecration, to further help you connect with Saint Joseph, we offer sections of prayers, information about service to others, and additional resources for more information on Saint Joseph. Finally, you may find brief information about the authors at the end of the book.

# Act of Consecration to Saint Joseph

Dear Saint Joseph,
God gave you the vocation and mission to be the husband of Mary, guardian of Jesus, protector of the Holy Family, and patron of the Church. I consecrate and entrust myself to you, and through you to Jesus, in every aspect of my daily life. I ask you to be my guardian and protector in all the trials, tribulations, and temptations of my life, as I follow Christ on the path to eternal life.

From the Lord, please obtain for me true humility of heart, purity of body, soul, and spirit, and a great love of God and my neighbor. By the grace of God, may all my thoughts, words, and actions—like yours and Mary's in the Holy Family—be completely dedicated to Jesus, now and always. Amen.

# The Complete Gospel Record of Joseph

*This 1952* RSV *translation was modified by Father Toschi.*

The book of the origin of Jesus Christ, the son of David, the son of Abraham. Abraham fathered Isaac, and Isaac fathered Jacob, and Jacob fathered Judah and his brothers, and Judah fathered Perez and Zerah by Tamar, and Perez fathered Hezron, and Hezron fathered Ram, and Ram fathered Amminadab, and Amminadab fathered Nahshon, and Nahshon fathered Salmon, and Salmon fathered Boaz by Rahab, and Boaz fathered Obed by Ruth, and Obed fathered Jesse, and Jesse fathered David the king. And David fathered Solomon by the wife of Uriah, and Solomon fathered Rehoboam, and Rehoboam fathered Abijah, and Abijah fathered Asa, and Asa fathered Jehoshaphat, and Jehoshaphat fathered Joram, and Joram fathered Uzziah, and Uzziah fathered Jotham, and Jotham fathered Ahaz, and Ahaz fathered Hezekiah, and Hezekiah fathered Manasseh, and Manasseh fathered Amos, and Amos fathered Josiah, and Josiah fathered Jechoniah and his brothers, at the time of the deportation to Babylon. And after the deportation to Babylon: Jechoniah fathered Shealtiel, and Shealtiel fathered Zerubbabel, and Zerubbabel fathered Abiud, and Abiud fathered Eliakim, and Eliakim fathered Azor, and Azor fathered Zadok, and Zadok fathered Achim, and Achim fathered Eliud, and Eliud fathered Eleazar, and Eleazar fathered Matthan, and Matthan fathered Jacob, and Jacob fathered Joseph, the husband of Mary, of whom Jesus was born, who is called Christ. So all the generations, from Abraham to David, were fourteen generations, and from David to the deportation to Babylon fourteen generations, and from the deportation to Babylon to the Christ fourteen generations. (Matthew 1:1–17.)

In the sixth month the Angel Gabriel was sent from God to a city of Galilee named Nazareth, to a virgin betrothed to a man whose name was Joseph, of the house of David; and the virgin's name was Mary. And he came to her and said, "Hail, O favored one, the Lord is with you!" But she was greatly troubled at the saying, and considered in her mind what sort of greeting this might be. And the angel said to her, "Do not be afraid, Mary, for you have found favor with God. And behold, you will conceive in your womb and bear a son, and you shall call his name Jesus. He will be great and will be called the Son of the Most High; and the Lord God will give to him the throne of his father, David, and he will reign over the house of Jacob for ever; and of his kingdom there will be no end." And Mary said to the angel, "How shall this be, since I do not know man?" And the angel said to her, "The Holy Spirit will come upon you, and the power of the Most High will overshadow you; therefore the child to be born will be called holy, the Son of God. And behold, your kinswoman Elizabeth in her old age has also conceived a son; and this is the sixth month with her who was called barren. For with God nothing will be impossible." And Mary said, "Behold, I am the handmaid of the Lord; let it be to me according to your word." And the angel departed from her. (Luke 1:26–38.)

Now the birth of Jesus Christ took place in this way. When his mother Mary had been betrothed to Joseph, before they came together she was found to be with child of the Holy Spirit; and her husband Joseph, being a just man and unwilling to put her to shame, resolved to divorce her quietly. But as he considered this, behold, an angel of the Lord appeared to him in a dream, saying, "Joseph, son of David, do not fear to take Mary your wife since that which is conceived in her is of the Holy Spirit; she will bear a son, and you shall call his name Jesus, for he will save his people from their sins." All this took place to fulfill what the Lord had spoken by the prophet: "Behold, a virgin shall conceive and bear a son, and his name shall be called Emmanuel" (which means "God with us"). When Joseph woke from sleep, he did as the angel of the Lord commanded him; he took his wife, but knew her not until she had borne a son; and he called his name Jesus. (Matthew 1:18–25.)

In those days a decree went out from Caesar Augustus that all the world should be enrolled. This was the first enrollment, when Quirinius was governor of Syria. And all went to be enrolled, each to his own city. And Joseph also went up from Galilee, from the city of Nazareth, to Judea, to the city of David, which is called Bethlehem, because he was of the house and lineage of David, to be enrolled with Mary, his betrothed, who was with child. And while they were there, the time came for her to be delivered. And she gave birth to her firstborn son and wrapped him in swaddling clothes, and laid him in a manger, because there was no place for them in the inn. And in that region there were shepherds out in the field, keeping watch over their flock by night. And an angel of the Lord appeared to them, and the glory of the Lord shone around them, and they were filled with fear. And the angel said to them, "Be not afraid; for behold, I bring you good news of great joy which will come to all the people; for to you is born this day in the city of David a Savior, who is Christ the Lord. And this will be a sign for you: you will find a babe wrapped in swaddling clothes and lying in a manger." And suddenly there was with the angel a multitude of the heavenly host praising God and saying, "Glory to God in the highest, and on earth peace among men with whom he is pleased!" When the angels went away from them into heaven, the shepherds said to one another, "Let us go over to Bethlehem and see this thing that has happened, which the Lord has made known to us." And they went with haste and found Mary and Joseph and the babe lying in a manger. And when they saw it they made known the saying which had been told them concerning this child; and all who heard it wondered at what the shepherds told them. But Mary kept all these things, pondering them in her heart. And the shepherds returned, glorifying and praising God for all they had heard and seen, as it had been told them. And at the end of eight days, when he was circumcised, he was called Jesus, the name given by the angel before he was conceived in the womb.

And when the time came for their purification according to the law of Moses, they brought him up to Jerusalem to present him to the Lord (as it is written in the law of the Lord, "Every male that opens the womb shall be called holy to the Lord") and to offer a sacrifice according to what is said in the law of the Lord, "a pair of turtledoves, or two young pigeons." Now there was a man in Jerusalem, whose name was Simeon, and this man was righteous and devout, looking for the consolation of Israel, and the Holy Spirit was upon him.

And it had been revealed to him by the Holy Spirit that he should not see death before he had seen the Lord's Christ. And inspired by the Spirit he came into the temple; and when the parents brought in the child Jesus, to do for him according to the custom of the law, he took him up in his arms and blessed God and said, "Lord, now let your servant depart in peace, according to your word; for my eyes have seen your salvation which you have prepared in the presence of all peoples, a light for revelation to the Gentiles, and for glory to your people Israel." And his father and his mother marveled at what was said about him; and Simeon blessed them and said to Mary his mother, "Behold, this child is set for the fall and rising of many in Israel, and for a sign that is spoken against (and a sword will pierce through your own soul also), that thoughts out of many hearts may be revealed." And there was a prophetess, Anna, the daughter of Phanuel, of the tribe of Asher; she was of a great age, having lived with her husband seven years from her virginity, and as a widow till she was eighty-four. She did not depart from the temple, worshiping with fasting and prayer night and day. And coming up at that very hour she gave thanks to God, and spoke of him to all who were looking for the redemption of Jerusalem. And when they had performed everything according to the law of the Lord, they returned into Galilee, to their own city, Nazareth. And the child grew and became strong, filled with wisdom; and the favor of God was upon him. (Luke 1:1–40.)

Now when [the magi] had departed, behold, an angel of the Lord appeared to Joseph in a dream and said, "Rise, take the child and his mother, and flee to Egypt, and remain there till I tell you; for Herod is about to search for the child, to destroy him." And he rose and took the child and his mother by night, and departed to Egypt, and remained there until the death of Herod. This was to fulfill what the Lord had spoken by the prophet, "Out of Egypt have I called my son." Then Herod, when he saw that he had been tricked by the wise men, was in a furious rage, and he sent and killed all the male children in Bethlehem and in all that region who were two years old or under, according to the time which he had ascertained from the wise men. Then was fulfilled what was spoken by the prophet Jeremiah: "A voice was heard in Ramah, wailing and loud lamentation, Rachel weeping for her children; she refused to be consoled, because they were no more." But when Herod died, behold, an angel of the Lord appeared in a dream to Joseph in Egypt, saying, "Rise, take the child and his mother, and go to the land of Israel, for those who sought the child's life are dead." And he rose and took the child and his mother, and went to the land of Israel. But when he heard that Archelaus reigned over Judea in place of his father Herod, he was afraid to go there, and being warned in a dream he withdrew to the district of Galilee. And he went and dwelt in a city called Nazareth, that what was spoken by the prophets might be fulfilled, "He shall be called a Nazorean." (Matthew 2:13–23.)

Now his parents went to Jerusalem every year at the feast of the Passover. And when he was twelve years old, they went up according to custom; and when the feast was ended, as they were returning, the boy Jesus stayed behind in Jerusalem. His parents did not know it, but supposing him to be in the company they went a day's journey, and they sought him among their kinsfolk and acquaintances; and when they did not find him, they returned to Jerusalem, seeking him. After three days they found him in the temple, sitting among the teachers, listening to them and asking them questions; and all who heard him were amazed at his understanding and his answers. And when they saw him they were astonished; and his mother said to him, "Son, why have you treated us so? Behold, your father and I have been looking for you anxiously." And he said to them, "How is it that you sought me? Did you not know that I must be in my Father's house?" And they did not understand the saying which he spoke to them. And he went down with them and came to Nazareth, and was obedient to them; and his mother kept all these things in her heart. And Jesus increased in wisdom and in stature, and in favor with God and man. (Luke 1:41–52.)

Now when all the people were baptized, and when Jesus also had been baptized and was praying, the heaven was opened, and the Holy Spirit descended upon him in bodily form, as a dove, and a voice came from heaven, "You are my beloved Son; with you I am well pleased." Jesus, when he began his ministry, was about thirty years of age, being the son (as was presumed) of Joseph. (Luke 3:21–23.)

Philip found Nathanael, and said to him, "We have found him of whom Moses in the law and also the prophets wrote, Jesus of Nazareth, the son of Joseph." Nathanael said to him, "Can anything good come out of Nazareth?" Philip said to him, "Come and see." (John 1:45–46.)

[Jesus] went away from there and came to his own country; and his disciples followed him. And on the Sabbath he began to teach in the synagogue; and many who heard him were astonished, saying, "Where did this man get all this? What is the wisdom given to him? What mighty works are wrought by his hands! Is not this the carpenter, the son of Mary...?" (Mark 6:1–3.)

And when Jesus had finished these parables, he went away from there, and coming to his own country he taught them in their synagogue, so that they were astonished, and said, "Where did this man get this wisdom and these mighty works? Is not this the carpenter's son?" (Matthew 13:53–55.)

And all spoke well of him, and wondered at the gracious words which proceeded out of his mouth; and they said, "Is not this Joseph's son?" (Luke 4:22.)

The Jews then murmured at him, because he said, "I am the bread which came down from heaven." They said, "Is not this Jesus, the son of Joseph, whose father and mother we know? How does he now say, 'I have come down from heaven?'" (John 6:41–42.)

# Prayers to Saint Joseph

## Prayer of Pope Leo XIII to Saint Joseph
*(To be said after the rosary)*

To you, O Blessed Joseph, we come in our trials, and having asked the help of your most holy spouse, we confidently ask your patronage, also. Through that sacred bond of charity which united you to the Immaculate Virgin Mother of God and through the fatherly love with which you embraced the Child Jesus, we humbly beg you to look graciously upon the beloved inheritance which Jesus Christ purchased by his blood, and to aid us in our necessities with your power and strength.

O most provident guardian of the Holy Family, defend the chosen children of Jesus Christ. Most beloved father, dispel the evil of falsehood and sin. Our most mighty protector, graciously assist us from heaven in our struggle with the powers of darkness. And just as you once saved the Child Jesus from mortal danger, so now defend God's Holy Church from the snares of her enemies and from all adversity. Shield each one of us by your constant protection so that, supported by your example and your help, we may be able to live a virtuous life, to die a holy death, and to obtain eternal happiness in heaven. Amen.

## Prayer of Pope Pius X to Saint Joseph the Worker

Glorious Saint Joseph, model of all who work, obtain for me the grace to work conscientiously, putting the call of duty above my many sins; to work with gratitude and joy, considering it an honor to employ and develop, by my labor, the gifts received from God; to work with order, peace, moderation and patience, never recoiling before weariness or difficulties; to work, above all, with pure intention and detachment from self, having always before my eyes death and the account which I must then render of time lost, of talents wasted, of good omitted, and of vain complacency in success, so fatal to the work of God. All for Jesus, all through Mary, all in imitation of you, O patriarch Joseph. This shall be my motto in life and death. Amen.

## Saint Joseph Rosary

This may be prayed just as a Marian rosary would, substituting the following prayer for the Hail Mary:

Joseph, son of David and husband of Mary. We honor you, guardian of the Redeemer, and we adore the Child you named Jesus.

Saint Joseph, patron of the universal Church, pray for us, that like you, we may live totally dedicated to the interests of the Savior.

## Mysteries

1. Betrothal to Mary (Matthew 1:18).
2. Annunciation to Joseph (Matthew 1:19–21).
3. Birth and naming of Jesus (Matthew 1:22–25).
4. Flight to Egypt (Matthew 2:13–15).
5. Hidden life at Nazareth (Matthew 2:23; Luke 2:51–52).

## Saint Joseph Novena

*Opening Prayer to Saint Joseph for Faith:*

Blessed Saint Joseph, heir of all the patriarchs, obtain for me this beautiful and precious virtue. Give me a lively faith, which is the foundation of all holiness, that faith without which no one can be pleasing to God. Obtain for me a faith that triumphs over all the temptations of the world and conquers human respect; a faith that cannot be shaken and that seeks God alone. In imitation of you, make me live by faith and submit my mind and heart to God, so that one day I may behold in heaven what I now firmly believe on earth.

*Day One: The Annunciation to the Betrothed Just Man*

First reading: Matthew 1:18–21
Second reading: John Paul II, *Redemptoris Custos*, sections 2–3
One or more decades of the Saint Joseph rosary (prayed as Marian rosary, substituting "Hail Mary" with "Joseph, son of David and husband of Mary"):

Joseph, son of David and husband of Mary; we honor you, guardian of the Redeemer, and we adore the Child you named Jesus. Saint Joseph, patron of the universal church, pray for us, that like you, we may live totally dedicated to the interests of the Savior.

### Day Two: Joseph Takes Mary, His Wife
First reading: Matthew 1:24
Second reading: John Paul II, *Redemptoris Custos*, section 20
One or more decades of the Saint Joseph rosary

### Day Three: The Birth and Naming of Jesus, Son of David
First reading: Matthew 1:16, 25
Second reading: John Paul II, *Redemptoris Custos*, sections 10, 12
One or more decades of the Saint Joseph rosary

### Day Four: The Presentation of Jesus, According to the Law of the Lord
First reading: Luke 2:22–40
Second reading: John Paul II, *Redemptoris Custos*, section 13
One or more decades of the Saint Joseph rosary

### Day Five: The Flight to Egypt
First reading: Matthew 2:13–15
Second reading: John Paul II, *Redemptoris Custos*, section 14
One or more decades of the Saint Joseph rosary

### Day Six: The Finding in the Temple and the Fatherhood of Joseph
First reading: Luke 2:41–52
Second reading: John Paul II, *Redemptoris Custos*, section 8
One or more decades of the Saint Joseph rosary

### Day Seven: Joseph the Worker
First reading: Matthew 13:53–55a
Second reading: John Paul II, *Redemptoris Custos*, sections 22, 24
One or more decades of the Saint Joseph rosary

### Day Eight: Patron of the Hidden and Interior Life
First reading Colossians 3:1–4
Second reading: John Paul II, *Redemptoris Custos*, sections 25–27d
One or more decades of the Saint Joseph rosary

### Day Nine: Patron and Model of the Church
First reading: 1 Corinthians 12:12, 27
Second reading: John Paul II, *Redemptoris Custos*, section 28, 30
One or more decades of the Saint Joseph rosary

NOTE: *Redemptoris Custos (Guardian of the Redeemer, Text and Reflections)* is also available from Guardian of the Redeemer publications at (831) 457-1868, or toll free at (866) 627-3556, or online at osjoseph.org.

## Daily Litany of Saint Joseph

| | |
|---|---|
| Lord, have mercy | *Lord, have mercy* |
| Christ, have mercy | *Christ, have mercy* |
| Lord, have mercy | *Lord, have mercy* |
| God the Father of Heaven | *have mercy on us* |
| God the Son, Redeemer of the world | *have mercy on us* |
| God the Holy Spirit | *have mercy on us* |
| Holy Trinity, one God | *have mercy on us* |
| Holy Mary | *pray for us* |
| Saint Joseph | *pray for us* |
| Noble son of David | *pray for us* |
| Light of patriarchs | *pray for us* |
| Husband of the Mother of God | *pray for us* |
| Chaste guardian of the Virgin | *pray for us* |
| Nurturing father of the Son of God | *pray for us* |
| Zealous defender of Christ | *pray for us* |
| Head of the Holy Family | *pray for us* |
| Joseph most just | *pray for us* |
| Joseph most chaste | *pray for us* |
| Joseph most prudent | *pray for us* |
| Joseph most strong | *pray for us* |
| Joseph most obedient | *pray for us* |
| Joseph most faithful | *pray for us* |
| Mirror of patience | *pray for us* |
| Lover of poverty | *pray for us* |
| Model for workers | *pray for us* |
| Splendor of family life | *pray for us* |
| Guardian of virgins | *pray for us* |
| Pillar of families | *pray for us* |

| | |
|---|---|
| Solace of the suffering | *pray for us* |
| Hope of the sick | *pray for us* |
| Patron of the dying | *pray for us* |
| Terror of demons | *pray for us* |
| Protector of Holy Church | *pray for us* |
| Lamb of God, who take away the sins of the world | *spare us, O Lord.* |
| Lamb of God, who take away the sins of the world | *hear us, O Lord.* |
| Lamb of God, who take away the sins of the world | *have mercy on us.* |
| He made him lord of his house | *and ruler of all his possessions.* |

Let us pray: O God, who in your inexpressible providence were pleased to choose Saint Joseph as spouse of the most holy Mother of your Son, grant, we pray, that we, who revere him as our protector on earth, may be worthy of his heavenly intercession.

Through our Lord Jesus Christ, your Son, who lives and reigns with you in the unity of the Holy Spirit, one God, for ever and ever. Amen.

## The Seven Sorrows and Joys of Saint Joseph

1. *Chaste lover of Mary, how overwhelmed you were when you thought that you would have to end your betrothal to her. But when the angel of God came to you in a dream, you were filled with awe to realize that Mary would be your wife, and you would be the guardian of the Messiah. Help us, Saint Joseph, help our families and all our loved ones to overcome all sadness of heart and develop an absolute trust in God's goodness.*

2. *Faithful guardian of Jesus, what a failure you thought you were when you could only provide a stable for the birth of the holy Child. And then what a wonder it was when shepherds came to tell of angel choirs, and the Wise Men came to adore the King of Kings. Through your example and prayers, help us, Saint Joseph, and all we love to become like sinless mangers where the Savior of the world may be received with absolute love and respect.*

3. *Tenderhearted Joseph, you also felt pain when the Blood of Jesus was first shed at his circumcision. Yet how proud you were to be the one privileged to give the name of Jesus, Savior, to the very Son of God. Pray for us, Saint Joseph, that the sacred Blood of Christ, poured out for our salvation, may guard our families so the divine name of Jesus may be written in our hearts forever.*

4. *Joseph, loving husband, how bewildered you were when Simeon spoke the words of warning that the hearts of Jesus and Mary would be pierced with sorrows. Yet his prediction that this would lead to the salvation of innumerable souls filled you with consolation. Help us, Saint Joseph, to see with eyes of faith that even the sorrows and pains of those we deeply love can become the pathway to salvation and eternal life.*

5. *Courageous protector of the Holy Family, how terrified you were when you had to make the sudden flight with Jesus and Mary to escape the treachery of King Herod and the cruelty of his soldiers. But when you reached Egypt, what satisfaction you had in knowing that the Savior of the world had come to replace the pagan idols. Teach us by your example, Saint Joseph, to keep far from the false idols of earthly attractions so that, like you, we may be entirely devoted to the service of Jesus and Mary.*

6. *Ever-obedient Joseph, you trustingly returned to Nazareth at God's command, in spite of your fear that King Herod's son might still be a threat to Jesus' life. Then what fatherly pride you had in seeing Jesus grow in wisdom and grace before God and men under your care. Show us, Saint Joseph, how to be free from all useless fear and worry, so we may enjoy the peace of a tranquil conscience, living safely with Jesus and Mary in our hearts.*

7. *Dependable father and husband, how anguished you and Mary were when, through no fault of yours, you searched for three days to find Jesus. What incredible relief was yours when you found him safe in the Temple of God. Help us, Saint Joseph, never to lose Jesus through the fault of our own sins. But if we should lose him, lead us back with unwearied sorrow until we find him again so that we, like you, may finally pass from this life, dying safely in the arms of Jesus and Mary.*

*And Jesus himself, when he began his work, was about thirty years old being, as was supposed, the son of Joseph.*

*Pray for us, holy Joseph.*
That we may be made worthy of the promises of Christ.

Let us pray: Blessed Saint Joseph, tenderhearted father, faithful guardian of Jesus, chaste spouse of the Mother of God, I pray and beseech you to offer to God the Father my praise to him through his divine Son, who died on the cross and rose again to give us sinners new life. Through the holy name of Jesus, pray with us that we may obtain from the eternal Father the favor we ask....(State your intention)....We have been unfaithful to the unfailing love of God the Father; beg of Jesus mercy for us. Amid the splendors of God's loving presence, do not forget the sorrows of those who suffer, those who pray, those who weep. By your prayers and those of your most holy spouse, our Blessed Lady, may the love of Jesus answer our call of confident hope. Amen.

These prayers and others are from the *Family of Saint Joseph Prayer Manual* (third edition), available from Guardian of the Redeemer Publications, 544 West Cliff Drive, Santa Cruz, California, 95060-6147, (831) 457-1868, toll free (866) 627-3556, osjoseph.org.

## Thirty Days Prayer to Saint Joseph

Ever blessed and glorious Joseph, kind and loving father, and helpful friend of all in sorrow! You are the good father and protector of orphans, the defender of the defenseless, the patron of those in need and sorrow. Look kindly on my request. My sins have drawn down on me the just displeasure of my God, and so I am surrounded with unhappiness. To you, loving guardian of the Family of Nazareth, do I go for help and protection.

Listen then, I beg you, with fatherly concern, to my earnest prayers, and obtain for me the favors I ask.

I ask it by the infinite mercy of the eternal Son of God, which moved him to take our nature and to be born into this world of sorrow.

I ask it by the weariness and suffering you endured when you found no shelter at the inn of Bethlehem for the holy Virgin, nor a house where the Son of God could be born. Then, being everywhere refused, you had to allow the queen of heaven to give birth to the world's Redeemer in a cave.

I ask it by the loveliness and power of that sacred name, Jesus, which you conferred on the adorable Infant.

I ask it by that painful torture you felt at the prophecy of holy Simeon, which declared the Child Jesus and his holy Mother future victims of our sins and of their great love for us.

I ask it through your sorrow and pain of soul when the angel declared to you that the life of the Child Jesus was sought by his enemies. From their evil plan you had to flee with him and his Blessed Mother to Egypt. I ask it by all the suffering, weariness, and labors of that long and dangerous journey.

I ask it by all your care to protect the sacred Child and his immaculate Mother during your second journey, when you were ordered to return to your own country. I ask it by your peaceful life in Nazareth where you met with so many joys and sorrows.

I ask it by your great distress when the adorable Child was lost to you and his Mother for three days. I ask it by your joy at finding him in the Temple, and by the comfort you found at Nazareth, while living in the company of the Child Jesus. I ask it by the wonderful submission he showed in his obedience to you.

I ask it by the perfect love and conformity you showed in accepting the divine order to depart from this life and from the company of Jesus and Mary. I ask it by the joy which filled your soul, when the Redeemer of the world, triumphant over death and hell, entered into the possession of his kingdom and led you into it with special honors.

I ask it through Mary's glorious assumption and through that endless happiness you have with her in the presence of God.

O good father! I beg you, by all your sufferings, sorrows, and joys, to hear me and obtain for me what I ask. (Here, state your petitions.)

Obtain for all those who have asked my prayers everything that is useful to them in the plan of God. Finally, my dear patron and father, be with me and all who are dear to me in our last moments, that we may eternally sing the praises of Jesus, Mary, and Joseph.

WITH PERMISSION OF THE SUPERIOR GENERAL OF THE JOSEPHITES

## Prayer for Vocations

Oh, Jesus, the Good Shepherd, when you saw your people abandoned like sheep without a shepherd you said, "The harvest is rich, but the laborers are scarce," and you urged us to pray to your heavenly Father to send workers to gather his harvest. Through the intercession of your most holy Mother Mary, Saint Joseph, and all the saints, graciously hear our prayer. Send to your Church many workers filled with zeal for the salvation of souls. Grant our request by the most precious Blood, which you shed for us and by the merits of your Sacred Heart. Amen.

# The Oblates of Saint Joseph

In Italy in 1878, Saint Joseph Marello founded the Oblates of Saint Joseph, a religious congregation of priests and brothers. He was inspired to gather a group of young men who desired to consecrate themselves to the love and service of Jesus in imitation of the prayerful, humble, and dedicated example of Saint Joseph. Saint Marello proposed a high ideal of an intense spiritual life united with a tremendous spirit of service. He viewed Saint Joseph as a pathway to holiness in which we can become "extraordinary in ordinary things," keeping before us the image of the young Jesus, simple, poor, and hidden, working for our salvation through the toil of everyday life. Joseph Marello was canonized on November 25, 2001.

The Oblates serve Jesus in whatever work is most necessary, without seeking to draw attention to themselves, working solely for the love of Christ. Saint Marello desired that they remain open to whatever missions Divine Providence sends their way, particularly assisting local churches most in need, the Christian education of young people, and leading people to Christ through the example of Saint Joseph. They began as a small community but have gradually grown and spread.

In 1915, the Holy Father requested that the Oblates begin apostolic services abroad, carrying devotion and the spirit of Saint Joseph throughout the world. At present, they are working in the following countries:

✦ Bolivia

✦ Brazil

✦ India

✦ Italy

✦ México

✦ Nigeria

✦ Peru

✦ The Philippines

✦ Poland

✦ The United States

## The Oblates Serve Christ Through:

1. Spreading devotion to Saint Joseph
2. Loyalty to the Holy Father and the teachings of the Catholic Church
3. Pastoral work in areas lacking of clergy
4. Christian formation and guidance of young people
5. Religious education
6. Catholic schools
7. Serving the elderly, immigrants, and the poor
8. Spiritual direction for retreats
9. Foreign missions

## Lay Associates

Associates to the Oblates of Saint Joseph are laymen and women (or diocesan priests) without profession of vows who choose to live a life of consecration to God and the Church in a spirit of collaboration with the Oblates. They take interest in the activities willed by Saint Marello and share in the spiritual benefits, rendering service within or outside the Oblate communities under the direction of the superior.

As associates, they live the spirituality of Saint Joseph according to the model of Saint Marello, join with the Oblates in prayer, and work closely with the Oblates in a number of areas, including:

1. Spreading devotion to Saint Joseph
2. Youth ministry
3. Parish ministry
4. Vocation ministry
5. Social apostolates
6. Missionary apostolates

The commitment to be a lay associate includes private consecration, with promises to serve God in imitation of Saint Joseph (humility, hidden life, hard work, and union with Jesus). The preparation of an associate in the Oblates of Saint Joseph will include learning to grow spiritually, ministering actively, and living a life of prayer and service.

## God's Call

It is the Lord who chooses and calls those whom he desires "… to follow more closely the divine Master" (Saint Marello). To help discover his call, men who sense a vocation to join the Oblates of Saint Joseph program as priests or brothers are encouraged to prayerfully consider the nature and purpose of their decision.

If you would like more information about the Oblates of Saint Joseph, please write to the Oblates of Saint Joseph, 544 West Cliff Drive, Santa Cruz, California 95060-6147, telephone (831) 457-1868, or send an e-mail to vocations@osjoseph.org. Also, you may visit the Oblates of Saint Joseph Web site at osjoseph.org.

# Additional Materials on Saint Joseph

## From LifeWork Press

If this book has inspired to you learn more about Saint Joseph and to become more like him in the many virtues he demonstrates, you will also enjoy the video *Joseph: The Man Closest to Christ.* This sixty-five-minute DVD presentation features insights and commentary from a variety of Catholic speakers and teachers and explores all aspects of Saint Joseph—the historical man, his response to God's call, and the many ways in which he reflects the nature of God.

A companion to this video presentation—*Tools From Joseph's Workshop: A 30-Day Apprenticeship With the Man Closest to Christ*—is also available. Written by Rick Sarkisian, PhD, this thirty-day men's devotional demonstrates the "tools" for building Joseph's virtues into your daily walk and becoming the authentic man God wants you to be.

Would you like to learn more about Joseph as a role model of authentic manhood? Read *Not Your Average Joe: The Real Saint Joseph and the Tools for Real Manhood in the Home, the Church and the World,* by Rick Sarkisian, PhD. This book is designed to present Joseph as he is and was—a rugged, hard-working man very much involved in the everyday life of his family and his world, a man with much to teach us about servanthood, integrity, and authentic manhood. This book will help you learn to make Joseph part of your daily life and to embrace the virtues that make him anything but "your average Joe."

*Joseph: The Man Closest To Christ, Tools From Joseph's Workshop,* and *Not Your Average Joe* are all part of the LifeWork Press library of life-purpose books and videos by Rick Sarkisian, PhD. Ask for a complete product brochure when you order!

To order any of these products, call toll-free (888) 297-4300 or visit lifeworkpress.com.

## From Guardian of the Redeemer Publications

*Guardian of the Redeemer* magazine is a quarterly publication of informative and inspirational material on Saint Joseph.

*Joseph in the New Testament,* by Father Larry Toschi, OSJ, is an in-depth study of the biblical texts on Saint Joseph.

*Saint Joseph in the Lives of Two Blesseds of the Church,* by Father Toschi, is a historical and spiritual study on the power of Saint Joseph in the lives of Blessed Junipero Serra and Saint Joseph Marello.

*Family of Saint Joseph Prayer Manual* is a booklet of prayers and devotions presented by the Oblates of Saint Joseph of California.

*Saint Joseph, Guardian of the Redeemer, Text and Reflections* is a book handsomely presenting Pope John Paul II's apostolic exhortation, along with the commentary of renowned Josephologist Father Tarcisio Stramare, OSJ.

*Saint Joseph Studies* is a collection of the papers presented in English at the international Saint Joseph symposia in Malta and El Salvador.

To order these and other Saint Joseph materials, such as prayer cards for the Holy Spouses Rosary, the Patron of the Unborn, or the Patron of the Dying, call toll-free (866) 627-3556, or visit osjoseph.org.

# About the Authors

**Father Larry Toschi, OSJ,** is pastor of Our Lady of Guadalupe Parish in Bakersfield, California, and founder of the Saint Joseph Bookstore and Art Exhibit at the Shrine of Saint Joseph, Guardian of the Redeemer in Santa Cruz, California. An Oblate of Saint Joseph since 1966, he has made presentations at international symposia on Saint Joseph since 1989. He is the author of *Joseph in the New Testament* and editor-in-chief of the quarterly periodical on Saint Joseph, *Guardian of the Redeemer.*

**Father José Antonio Bertolin, OSJ,** is director of the Josephite-Marellian Spirituality Center in Apucarana, Paraná, Brazil. He has published many books on Saint Joseph and edits the monthly Saint Joseph magazine *Estudos Josefinos.* He organizes national study weeks on Saint Joseph. He is also vice provincial of the Brazilian province of the Oblates of Saint Joseph, the director of São José School, and the rector of the community of the Saint Joseph Shrine parish in Apucarana.

**Rick Sarkisian, PhD,** is a nationally known life-purpose author, conference speaker, and video producer who has helped thousands of people seek and understand their purpose in life. In addition to working closely with the Oblates of Saint Joseph, Rick writes for a variety of Christian publications and is a frequent guest on nationally broadcast radio and television shows. Rick and his wife, Cheryl, have been married since 1979 and have five children.